Congratulations—

Forsaking all others you have discovered and chosen each other. You stand now on the threshold of the "long adventure that is Christian marriage."

In a desire to speak sensibly of changeless things in these days of rapid change, this booklet has been re-written numerous times in a dozen years. The insights and comments of countless young couples have, we hope, kept its message alive. Your suggestions too, would be deeply appreciated.

We hope the chapters that follow may be of service. You have already fashioned a strong bond between you, but there is still much to be learned, lived and loved since,

> "Love is an activity, not a passion . . .
> its essence is to 'labor,' 'to make
> someone grow.' To love a person
> productively implies to care and to feel
> responsible for his life, growth and the
> development of all his human powers."

CONTENTS

*"Everything you never wanted to ask
about theology but darn well ought to . . .
if the Good News of the Gospel is to have
any meaning in your life and marriage
beyond that of rules and prohibitions."*

*"Twenty-five thousand quickly fleeting days
—that's one lifetime. Is that all there is?"*

*"I have come that you might have life
more richly and abundantly."*

The People Of God

Man is the only animal that knows he is going to die, the only one who asks, "What is it really about?"

Only man can shape his future, can put the question, "What is truly important for me to think, to do and to become when I dare reflect that I won't be around very long?"

Some people ask, "What has religion to do with my daily life? How is it relevant to my happiness? Well, whenever man ponders the ultimate questions of life, death and meaning, whenever he asks, "How shall I live, what shall I do to find fulfillment?", he is already in the realm of religion.

RELIGION IS MYTH AND VISION

Religion is man's attempt to find answers to the key questions of life. It is also his fidelity to living honestly by the light of the insights he discovers. Religion is myth, not as in legend or fable, but myth as a deeper kind of knowing. Religion as myth is an organized insight and intuition about man's origin

1

and destiny beyond and above scientific knowledge. It is the basic story which tells what he is about as he attempts to learn reality and come in touch with God.

Religion is also a vision of an ideal way of life constantly challenging man against fear and selfishness to become his better truer self. A church is a body of people who share the same religious vision and tradition.

We who share the Judaeo-Christian heritage believe that the answer to ultimate questions are found in an infinite, Creator-God who broke into human history and into the consciousness of mankind in a process called Revelation. As we reach adulthood, the simplistic conceptions of this God and His workings—the bearded old man in the cloud shaping up the lives of a handful of Hebrew shepherds—must give way to richer theological insights that carry more meaning.

If the universe has been exploding into space at the speed of light for millions of years, theology challenges us with the realization that beyond all, beyond the farthest borders of space, and within all, at the very source and ground of life is a God who is infinite being, totally other and yet Father of all.

What meaning does He have for you?

HOW GOD RELATES TO LIFE

The events in the book of Exodus tell us how Yahweh brought the Jewish nation out of bondage in Egypt and proclaimed Himself to them.

"If now you listen to Me and keep My covenant then out of all the nations you shall become My special possession. You shall be My holy people." This was the testament, the covenant, the agreement, the forming of the chosen people to whom God promised a glorious destiny. But the old covenant was only a beginning, "In the latter day God sent His only Son to call forth a new people, a priestly people, a church, a community of saints."

But why the formation of a special people? Because mankind created with freedom was also beset with an original weakness, an original flaw—SELF-CENTEREDNESS.

Two years ago January I foolishly made a commitment to give a series of talks in a monastery four hundred miles from my home during the following July. As the date approached, busy with other things, I became irritated at the prospect of having to "waste" three days of my crowded schedule.

Four days before I was scheduled to leave, I got a phone call from the prior of the monastery, "Listen, next week's seminar has been called off. Father George (he was running the show) just got word that his mother, father and sister were killed in a highway accident back in Missouri." I put down the phone with a sense of relief and called to the man in the next office, "Hey, good news! I don't have to go." A friend of mine had lost his family and I named it "good news."

The basic flaw and challenge of the human condition is right there. Man presuming that he is the center and lord of creation, that what pleases him is all important. A pebble in my shoe is "more serious and important" than a thousand Pakistani starving to death after flood and earthquake. Man afraid to let go and to be for others. It is the healing of this primeval wound of selfishness that requires a love people.

THE CHURCH IS A LOVE STORY

If you would want to understand the church, look at its origins. In the earliest days after the Resurrection when the Holy Spirit, the Spirit of love, descended on a small band of men and women gathered around the Apostles, this was the church, the people of God. Our word, "church," is laden with so many memories and meanings for each of us that some of the earlier terms used speak to us more clearly. There is the Hebrew word, *qahod,* the "assembly of the people," or better the Greek word, *ecclesia* which means a people especially called forth.

The original church looked quite different from the one we know. There were no dioceses or catechisms, no religious orders or confessionals, no code of canon law and in those early days, no buildings. Yet church was essentially there for church is not buildings or structures or legal codes. The church is a people, a people who saw a vision, listened to a love story, believed and became a community of lovers in Christ.

3

WHO IS HOLY?

Why did God choose to form a special, holy people? Let's unpack the word "holy." "Holy" in theology means being like God. That idea doesn't help very much for too many of us have strange, almost childish conceptions of God. To some He is the "teddy bear God" who consoles us. Like Linus' blanket He is a security symbol we cling to. He will make everything all right regardless of how we live our lives. God and I have a deal. God understands and excuses all. In my last moments the pink angel will come and carry me above the clouds.

For others He is "the mad scientist" or "thunderbolt God," the "spy in the sky who knows our every thought and inmost desires." He has given us rules, laws and distasteful tasks and watches us perform like mice in a maze. When we fail a test he calls it sin and drops us into hell.

These inadequate, folkloric conceptions of God make it very difficult for Him to have meaning in our daily lives. If holiness is being like God, who can identify with a blanket, a teddy bear or a mad scientist?

Well, what then do we truly know about God? Only what He has revealed. Scripture insistently tells us: God is love.

"God is love and he who abides in love abides in God and God in him."

God is three persons: Father, Son and Holy Spirit caught up in the eternal embrace of interpersonal love. God is a community of love. The very essence of God is love in relationship. Thus if the word holy means being like God, it means being a lover. It means one who can forget self and reach out and relate to others in love—one who creates love.

Holy does *not* mean standing pale and bloodless in a stained glass window with a lily in your hand. It does not mean being aloof, withdrawn, afraid to become contaminated by the world. Holiness, whether said of Francis of Assisi or John XXIII, Martin Luther King or Albert Schweitzer is always the same. It means being like God, a tremendous, passionate lover committed to flesh and blood people in the real world. Christians are to be the love people.

THE VISION

How do you make a people? You do it with a vision. Lombardi made the Green Bay Packers with a vision of excellence. Washington, Adams and Jefferson called forth the American people with a vision of a new nation dedicated to liberty, equality and justice for all. Hitler created the Nazi party with a vision that said, "You are the supermen who must rule the world." You make a people with a vision they can share and a spirit that unites and enthuses them.

Let's go back to those earliest Christians. We listed all the things they did not have. What was the vision they did have which made them a people, a church? They had the experience of the Christ—the words, the promises, the living, vibrant presence of the God-man who slept with them, fished with them, ate, laughed, talked and sang with them. In Himself he revealed the ultimate meaning of life, a revolutionary vision.

He said startling things like if someone strikes you on the side of the face, turn the other cheek. If a thief takes your coat, run after him and give him your raincoat, too. He said if you love those who love you, that's no great trick. The pagans do that. He said the Christian challenge is to be an initiator of love —to love the unlovable, to love your enemies, to love one another, to forgive innumerable times, even to lay down your life for a friend. He told them the crucial secret contained in the Easter mystery: that life comes through death. If we are to find the richness and fullness of life we must die to self and risk ourselves in loving others.

BREAKTHROUGH

Be careful. We are not here repeating the meekness routine you heard in fourth grade. It is not the Christian's mission to become doormat to the world or to buy a big sign to hang on his back that says "Kick me, I'm a Christian." No, Christ was talking about something far more psychologically authentic.

Take Joey. He's seven. His parents have had him take swimming lessons all summer. He's learned to swim but there he is, poised at the edge of the pool afraid to dive—scared stiff.

The instructor knows he's ready, so he sneaks up behind him, gives him a push and in he dives. All of a sudden Joey enjoys it. The fear is gone. He climbs out, dives in, out, in repeatedly for the sheer pleasure of it until his mother says, "It's time to go home." He has come to a breakthrough experience, enjoying a whole new level of activity and sensation that he would never have known unless forced to overcome his fears.

Take the self-centered young man who meets the right girl. She unlocks him. The center of his concern moves outside himself and, in love, he begins to live more fully and intensely. The Lord is telling us that the key to life is the leap of faith and the thrust of love.

If we can forget our anxieties, hangups about our status, our comfort, our point of view, our image, our power to control and manipulate people,—if we can reach out to them in friendship and love, we will come to a rewarding break-through experience that brings fulfillment in rich relationships.

THE IMPOSSIBLE DREAM

The Lord gave the earliest Christians (and us) a vision of what the world might be without fear, hatred, self-interest, cruelty or pettiness. They were intoxicated with the vision and we should be, too. He told men that they were not alone, that they were all sons of God and, therefore, brothers. He promised that to as many as would believe and become baptized (that is, become one of the special people) he would send the spirit of love to motivate them and make them a community. He challenged them to dream the impossible dream of the world not as it is, but as it could be with peace, justice, mutual concern and the spirit of love. He commanded them to go forth and to share his vision with all men, to be lovers, to do the works of love, to witness, to love and to transform the face of the earth.

WHY CHURCH?

All right, so we have a vision and a challenge of love, but why do we need a church? Can't people be saved without any formal connection to the organized, institutional church? The answer, of course, is yes. As St. Augustine put it,

"There are many in the church who do not belong to God and many who belong to God who are not in the church." Then why bother with the formal church?

Try this analogy. There were conservationists, pollution fighters and anti-pollution feelings long before Earth Day, Paul Erlich or Ralph Nader came on the scene. However, once the threat to environment became greater the anti-pollution cause became dramatized. It became a visible movement. Interested people could identify others who shared their vision. Knowledge and resources could be pooled, plans developed, the public educated, converts made, enthusiasm stirred. There was now a people dedicated to the fight.

Long before Christ there was love in the world. But Christ came to dramatize love, to tell us that growing out of selfishness to love was at the center of reality, to give us a new way of seeing life with love at its core. "If you would find your lives, you must have a change of heart. Pour out your lives in love then you will find life more abundantly."

The church is the visible group of people who accept this vision of love. Notice, we are talking about those Christians who really (committedly) "buy in on the gut level."

There may be great lovers outside the church just as there may be great pollution fighters outside the movement. But the church is the visible, formal group of people blessed with, challenged with, stuck with the task of exploring the vision of total love—of studying it, living it, bearing witness to it, attracting others to it and bringing it to bear on the needs of every age and culture. Christians, the love people, are a light, a yeast and a leaven to renew the world. Christians are the ones who are fated to re-discover, re-live and re-tell the love story in every age of the world, "until He comes again."

LITURGY AND THE EXPERIENCE OF LOVE

Only those who have experienced the transforming power of love are impelled to do something about it. The role of the liturgy is to continually form the community by steeping it in the vision of love, by re-presenting the story of the God-man who loved so much that the made a free decision to die in order to prove his love. Why all the recent changes in the liturgy? To make us realize that we do not go to church to be passive spectators watching something happening up front.

"Liturgy is the source and font of the Christian life." Why? How? Take an example: the sports arena, Nurenburg, Germany, the year is 1934. Over 200,000 Nazis at the Party rally, a most grotesque yet effective "liturgy." Hundreds of searchlights, thousands of banners with the swastika on the blood-red field, the ancient symbol reviving primitive pagan memories of the Teutonic people. The sea of torches in the dusk. Uniforms, swirling brown and black shirts. Brass bands blaring incessantly. The young people chanting the "Horst Wessel" song . . . and the leader proclaiming their destiny. His maniacal, hypnotizing voice magnified through a thousand loudspeakers. Then the responsory, the rolling waves of the Nazi salute, "Seig Heil! Seig Heil!", roaring from 200,000 throats. In this mass frenzy, this "liturgy," people experienced themselves as the *obermensch,* the supermen. They rushed forth transformed, dedicated to changing the face of Europe for a thousand years. They were a people aware of themselves in a special way, feeling power, burning with a cause.

The Nazi liturgy was a false liturgy. It betrayed its participants and led them and the world to a bloodbath— to horror and tragedy. But the point of the example is to show how liturgy can effect real change, can make a vision into a reality, can inspire and transform.

THERE ARE NO OTHERS

The Christian liturgy is based on the reality of God and the human person's need to become a lover. Its purpose is to tell us who we are. To celebrate, that is to dramatize repeatedly, the most important events of our salvation history and to steep us in the word of God.

When you and some friends go to the lake shore, light a fire, drink some beer, sing the old songs, re-tell the old stories, that is a good "liturgy." You end up more friends than before. You experience each other.

As one older priest put it, "When I get to be pastor, I'm going to make every person in church wear name tags. We're going to have discussions before Mass, coffee after Mass and wine in the basement when we can afford it so that the people of the parish get to know each other, to build up bonds of intimacy and trust, so they begin to care about each other and experience support and friendship."

The only people we ever hate are "other" people, the minority groups who threaten our jobs and neighborhoods, strangers who threaten our security or self-esteem. We can only dislike people when we see them as "other," as alien, as foreign to ourselves. Even when the husband and wife have a quarrel and one or the other complains, "He takes me for granted," "She doesn't understand me," the marriage counselor describes them as alienated.

The liturgy tries to make us understand and re-experience the fact that there are no "other" people, no strangers in the community of love. We are all brothers, we are all one, we are all redeemed and transformed in the blood of Christ.

Scripture tells us of the man who looks in the mirror but turning away, soon "forgets what manner of man he is." Today, with the frantic pace of our busy lives, it is so easy to forget that we are part of the love people, easy to slip back into self-centeredness, totally absorbed in our own world, captives of our own feelings. In the liturgy, as we listen, pray, speak, sing, and eat together, we find our truest identity. We acknowledge that we are not God, not the center of all and that we must return to God through our fellow man.

THE SACRAMENTS

Christ and His church, His people, are *the* great sacrament, that is, the great symbol and cause of redemptive, altruistic love at work in the world. There are seven other signs that put us in touch with God's love that we also call sacraments. Remember, "A sacrament is an outward sign instituted by Christ to give grace?" It's time we took this basically good grammar school definition and understood its deeper meanings.

Why should we receive sacraments? To get more grace, we were told. But grace is not a thing. Receiving grace is not like putting anti-freeze in the Chevrolet to get it through the winter, six quarts are good, but eight are better because it might be very cold. Grace is no-thing, not anti-freeze or electrical energy or a stimulant drug that turns us on.

Sacraments are not magic. Some used to feel that if the priest were in sin but said the words of consecration correctly, and if the recipient were mostly asleep but safely got the host in his mouth, something wonderful happened when really nothing much happened at all. For the grace of God must work through the minds, hearts and attitudes of men.

LOVE PRESENCE

Try this approach. What changes people? Every fall students get fresh notebooks and vow that this semester, by sheer will power, they're going to get everything on paper and keep on top of all their subjects. But little changes. By Thanksgiving day they are scrambling again. The same is mostly true of resolutions made at New Year's or after a retreat. Little really changes. We are changed, we grow and develop when we are exposed to the loving presence of another person.

The maladjusted boy from the terrible home situation comes to a special school and the teacher-psychologist works with him. She is patient with his tantrums, puts her arms around him when he cries, applauds when he draws a straight line. She gives him a concentrated experience of care and love. Slowly, like the heat and light of the summer sun opening a bud to full bloom, her love presence opens the child. It unlocks his personality. He puts aside fears and begins to risk meeting life. Her love has "convinced him" that he is worthwhile. He is "created" in love.

God is always present to us in His once-and-for-all creative art of love and providence. He is with mankind. Christ is always changelessly, existentially present to us. The sacraments are special, ritual moments wherein we can open ourselves to His always available love, when we, depending on our faith and fervor, can encounter Christ.

10

Some people have the conception when they go to confession, God, Who is taking His ease up in heaven is nudged by St. Peter. He looks down, points His finger and ZAPS grace into us. That's not the way it is. Theology tells us that God is changeless, He is always loving, always present. In the sacraments the change takes place within us. It can be understood as a qualitative change within us, an intensification of love, a deeper understanding of faith, of who we are and what we are for, a greater dedication to God and our fellow men. The sacraments are symbolic meeting points, encounters with God's loving presence.

SYMBOL OF REALITY

Sacraments are symbols or signs. They work as symbols and symbols are real.

You have a lawn so maybe you put up a sign that says, "Keep dogs off the grass." Now if your neighbor walks his dog across the grass you can go out and point to the sign. He reads it and takes his dog off the grass. In this instance the sign is working as sign. On the other hand, you could run out, pick up the sign and hit both neighbor and dog across the head with it. In this case the sign is not working as sign, it's working as club.

The sacraments work as signs or symbols and in this sense they are deeply human. Take the American taboo that says no one may speak in a crowded elevator. There are sixteen people crowded together shoulder-to-shoulder, touching each other. But they are not really present to each other in any human sense, because their minds and emotions are not involved with each other and there is no communication. They are rather like bowling balls on a rack. In one corner of the elevator you have a boy from the stock room. In another corner, 8 feet away, a girl from the typing pool. She smiles and he nods and he waves his head in a way that says clearly, at least to her, "Come on. Let's have a cup of coffee." She nods her agreement. They have exchanged symbols yet their contact is far more human, far deeper, far more real than that of the people touching each other in the middle of the elevator.

Man receives all his knowledge, all the information that stirs his emotions through symbols—words, touches, sounds. This is the only way he can truly be communicated with on the human level. It is the only way God can communicate with him.

SYMBOLS CARRY POWER

Signs and symbols carry power even over time and space. Your parents may, like you, have some special song that meant a great deal to their courtship. It may have been Glenn Miller or Johnny Ray or the young Frank Sinatra singing "That Old Black Magic." If, on their twenty-fifth wedding anniversary mother sneaks out the old record and plays it for your dad, the symbol that leaps over a quarter of a century carries memories of young love, dedication, early excitement or dreams in a time when life was new, and carrying these meanings it has the power to move daddy right now. It can touch them both and cause change in them both. It can make them more warm and sensitive and loving.

Try another example. The summer before he died, John Kennedy stood on the Kurfurstendamm in Berlin during the crisis, before almost 200,000 people. With that characteristic chopping gesture and the familiar nasal voice filled with emotion, he said, "If standing here on the brink of danger is what it means to be a free man, *ich bin ein Berliner.*" "I, too will be a Berliner." If you're not too old or too disillusioned and you are put in touch with that symbol, hearing it on radio or seeing the film clip, you can still be stirred by the image of those, "Years of Lightning, Days of Drums," when hope flourished in the land and the grace and style of the young president touched us all and made us confident that we could face all of the tomorrows. John Kennedy existed. The Kennedy event took place. When we are put in touch with it, it still has the power to stir us deeply.

Christ existed. The Christ events took place. When we can symbolically be put in touch with them, they carry power. They can stir us if we but open our minds and hearts to the encounter with the love story.

Perhaps the best analogy for sacrament is a kiss. George and Susan go out on a date. He is mostly shy but also proud that she is with him because she is very lovely. They eat, drink, dance and talk, become interested in and respond to each other. He talks and she listens. She talks and he agrees warmly. He's feeling expansive. He's never been this free and comfortable with anyone before and he takes her home wondering, "Does she really like me?" On her front porch he wonders, is this the beginning of something? Should I kiss her, shouldn't I kiss her? Finally, plucking up his courage he kisses her tenderly *and she kisses back*. And in this symbol he finds meaning. "Yes, she did enjoy herself. Yes, she really did like me." The symbol seals and confirms and proves the interest and love relationship that is beginning to bud between them. But the kiss also looks to the future and leads him to say, "Yes, this can be good. I will call her again tomorrow." Not only does the kiss confirm what went before, but it also deepens their relationship and *causes* more interest and more of a bond between them.

The sacraments, too, are not only *signs* of divine love, they also *cause* change and growth because they lead the mind and emotions of the believer to be more deeply and fully immersed in the Gospel mystery, in God's love presence, His grace.

SEVEN SIGNS OF LOVE

In Christ, God became visible to man. Christ was the sign, the word of the Father. In His people, His Church, Christ (and hence God) remained visible to all of us through history, and the Church in turn becomes visible in the seven sacramental signs. Through them we are in a special way touched by and put in touch with the reality of Christ.

From time immemorial men have given the high points of existence a dramatic and significant (sign carrying) form . . . birth, death, the banquet, forgiveness, coming of age, and taking on crucial life vocations such as marriage and priestly service. These key events are signaled by celebration which contrasts them with the ordinariness of daily life and underlines their importance.

It was these very key points of existence that Christ named sacraments so that in addition to their earthly meanings they would also tell us about the deepest meaning of reality—that life is about loving, that we can become fully human only through the challenge and inspiration of divine love presence.

Baptism is initiation into the love community. The baptized adult says in effect, "I accept the understanding of existence which Christ holds forth and commit myself to His community of love and its works in the world."

Confirmation is like a rite of passage. In adolescence an Indian boy was put through ordeals and ceremonies to signify his movement into manhood. He was then no longer a child, a taker in the tribe, being cared for and fed by adults. He now had new status, to be warrior and hunter, to serve the tribe. Confirmation is a challenge to the young person to enter the fullness of Christian life, the active task of loving and serving.

Penance is reconciliation to Christ and His community. The one who has done harm repents and is brought back into the network of love relationships.

In the Final Anointing, as man confronts the cosmic mystery, the "great perhaps" of life after death, he is readied and reassured that this is no end but the real beginning of life in eternal love.

In the Eucharist, the Christian community shares the body of Christ as food. The sharing of food was to primitive man the highest love act. He did not have plentiful stores layed up in bin or freezer. He lived on the edge of starvation. When he gave up food, he was hazarding his own survival for the good of another. It is this tremendous love act to which Christ has attached His free "giving up of Himself unto death." In the Eucharist the Christian says, "I will nourish my spirit and try to live up to this ideal of love strong as death."

Priesthood is the designation of certain persons in the community to learn, to live and to tell over again the love story of Christianity, to minister to the people in order that they might remember who they are.

Marriage is the sacrament of human love and service to new life, the sacrament of dedicated, faithful love of one man for one woman who commit themselves to each other's full growth until death do them part, and to nurturing and raising children to personhood in the Christian vision.

"Sacrament is an encounter with Christ."

"Two people who marry in Christ become a sacrament."

Symbol, Sign, Sacrament

If there were no such nation as the United States, what we call the American flag would still be a beautiful piece of cloth, but it would not be a symbol that carried meaning or power. The flag, to be a symbol, must stand for the country, its people, their traditions and dreams. If there were no Gospel, no Christian people, no Church, marriage would still be a natural institution (as it was for centuries before Christ), but it would not be a sacrament, a symbol that carried special meaning and power. As flag must be understood in terms of country, so the sacrament must be thought of in the context of the Church.

Marriage and the other sacraments are signs and causes of Christ's redemptive love at work in the world. They are the retelling and the re-living of the Gospel vision of love.

BELIEF SHAPES LIFE

How does a couple, the Browns, who enter a sacramental marriage differ from the Greens who do not? Do the "sacramental" Browns look or act differently from the "secular" Greens? Is it possible that the Greens might be better people than the Browns? What in fact does the dimension "sacramental" add to a marriage?

A person shapes his life and behavior by what he believes and loves. A man convinced he is Napoleon may spend every day, hand in vest giving orders to imaginary armies. If the convictions of one individual shape and form his life, then the convictions of two people who marry give a special quality to their relationship, their marriage. If both partners share similar, deep convictions, these reinforce each other and become a truly important factor in setting the character of the marriage.

Two practicing Birchites might spend their honeymoon hunting Communists under beds, while two dedicated SDS members might spend theirs making bombs. Two selfish people might strive to see how much they could own by their fifth anniversary; two service-oriented people might join the Peace Corps.

Two committed Christians are possessed of a special faith vision which influences and gives particular form and quality to their marriage. We are talking about real believers not nominal, marginal Christians, not about the couple, who when asked, "Why do you want to be married in the Church?", say "It really doesn't matter to us, but our mothers prefer it that way." For this couple, sacrament is empty ritual and church ceremony is simply a nice, acceptable social custom.

CHRISTIAN INTENTIONALITY

Two people more truly Christian share a package of beliefs, attitudes, hopes and desires which give special character to their marriage. To a greater or lesser degree, they would believe:

—In a reality beyond the here and now.

—That they were challenged to serve each other forever with an unselfish, mysterious, sometimes even sacrificial love that goes beyond the logic of the psychologists.

—That the Church, the people of God, is a community of believers, keepers of the LOVE STORY, to whom they can turn for vision and support.

—That their marriage relationship is designated to be an effective sign by repeating and re-presenting the Gospel Love Story in miniature for the inspiration of their brothers and all men. This is precisely why St. Paul calls marriage a high mystery having to do with Christ and His Church.

What is different about the "sacramental" Browns? The theologians would call it "Christian intentionality." Their minds and hearts are both open and imprinted in such a way that they live in the context of the Christian message.

"They affirm what Jesus and His Gospel embody and convey the basic meaning and direction of human life and all reality; that in Christ we find a shouted, ringing 'NO!' to the sad question asked in Peggy Lee's sick little song, 'Is That All There Is?'—No! That's not all there is. . . . You shall have life and have it more abundantly!"

Have you ever read an essay and found it difficult and confusing and then, suddenly, you come upon a crucial sentence or a key definition that clarifies the whole thing and makes it fall into place? For the "sacramental" Browns, Christ is the answer to the mystery of existence. He is the light, the key to meaning and reality, the key that unlocks them to grow beyond their fears to become their best selves, to become fully human.

THE SACRAMENT BEGINS

The sacrament of matrimony begins when a couple stands "In the sight of God and in the face of this company," and declares, in some form, "We take each other for better or for worse . . . till death do us part." *Notice, when they do this they are not in fact starting a love relationship. They have presumably been in love with each other for months or even years.* No! What they *are doing* is announcing, describing, and dedicating their relationship. They are making it a sacrament. They are becoming a sacrament, the public sign and cause of redemptive love to each other, their children, and fellow men.

They are in fact saying something joyous, yet awesome:

"Whatever befalls we are going to mingle our two lives completely into one, together, forever; to live, love, and grow, together, forever; to raise children; to build a family, to serve God and man from this new nuclear community of love."

They are crying out,

"Whoever I am, whatever I can become, I give to you. I want to discover myself with you and through you, and I will try to summon forth the best self that is in you."

They are shouting,

"People, we believe in the foolish, glorious, Christian vision, the impossible dream that if we pour our lives out for each other, we'll each possess life more richly. We have the courage to try to imitate and live the Gospel Love Story. We want you characters who call yourselves Christians to know about it, to take heart from us, to be inspired by the fact that we are willing to hazard ourselves on the fact that this vision is reality, is what life is all about, and will bring us to happiness here and hereafter."

And, finally, they are saying,

"We do this as part of the Christian community and we need your help, support, friendship, your discipline, prayers, and presence, to make this dream work."

SACRAMENT TO EACH OTHER

To the extent that any one person can enter into, touch and shape the unique personhood of another, in marriage you are invited and committed to do just that, to assume responsibility for the growth and destiny of your spouse. You are commissioned to call forth the best that is in him or her. This is your task. This is your challenge.

Years of thought and research, millions of dollars and rooms full of complex medical equipment all focus down into the tip of a radium needle which touches the malignant spot in one individual's body to heal and make him whole. For your fiance, God's providential love, Christ's eternal plan of redemption, the Gospel vision, is focused and concentrated in and through you. In marriage you are the contact point; you stand as the personification of Christ's love for your partner. You are irrevocably designated, commissioned, ordained, to redeem him or her, to bring him to the fullness of life. You are the ministers and bearers of the sacrament to each other.

WHO IS "BETTER?"

In marriage, the "sacramental" couple encounters Christ in a special way. They are challenged by Him to make a total gift of self and to grow in the process. They are to be Christ's love-presence, the vehicle of His grace, one to the other.

Given all this, could the secular Browns still be "better" people than those found in some sacramental marriages? Of course. If by training and heritage they have been brought up to a significant level of love, virtue, and service, they could be "better" than mechanical, name-only, Christians.

God is not limited by our conceptions of Him. He is not constrained to operate merely in the ways we understand or think proper—to run on tracks that we have laid in our minds. "God writes straight with crooked lines," sometimes exceedingly crooked.

CHRIST THE KEY

Again, what's different about the "sacramental" Browns? Their belief in Christ. They can be, depending on their faith commitment, more full of humanity because they are in touch with divine love.

St. Irenaeus said in the third century, "Man fully human is God's greatest glory." The ideal human person is the one who can love most unselfishly. For believers, Christ is the ideal, the model, the paradigm. To the extent that we become more fully human, more wise, mature, emotionally balanced, more generous and loving, we become more Christ-like, more holy, more like the "man for others" in whom divinity and humanity were met. Left to himself, man's tendencies toward self-centeredness, his fears for his self-image, and the aggressions and manipulations he will resort to, to maintain himself as the center of creation, prevent him from breaking through to the fully human. Man needs the faith-vision, the challenge of God's grace in Christ to help him to be what he could be.

"In the sacrament, the conjugal love of the couple is mingled with, assumed into, supercharged by the love of Christ.

"It is in this love—and now a decisive word must be spoken, the one word which can really place us in the New Testament—that the cross has its place. Thus it is a love which is proof against disappointment, a loyalty which is proof against failure—failure to come up to each other's expectations, to make joy full, to find love satisfying. It is love and loyalty which persist even where humanly speaking there seems to be no reason for it—just as the cross of Jesus was hopeless until it brought joy, salvation and new life.

"Christ's love presence in marriage does not mean that
there will not be clashes of temperament, mistakes in choice
of partner, troubles with children, strained nerves, illness,
boredom and even necessary and final separation. But it does
mean that for Christians there is always a further dimension
of love present which strengthens, consoles, and gives hope".

THE SACRAMENT IN BEING

How do the partners bring Christ's love presence, one to the
other? Not by being pietistic, or burdening their days with
sweet religious practices. No, the focusing of Christ's love is far
more humanly realistic. The couple perfect each other because
marriage is a school of love.

At the outset of life, the infant knows nothing but himself.
It takes him months to figure out the smooth one is momma, the
rough one, papa. His task and preoccupation is survival.
Concerned only with himself, he is a taker, a crying insistent
demander. But slowly, after years of constant love, service . . .
food, cuddling, praise are provided by his parents, he begins
to trust. "If these two take so much time and trouble with me,"
he says, "they must like me. I must be lovable." He begins to
gain confidence, to open to interaction with others. Thus the
family, THE FIRST SCHOOL OF LOVE, has loved him into the
earliest stages of personhood.

In adolescence, his friends, peer group, teachers continue to
school him in love. He learns that his competencies, his attitudes
and he, himself, are appreciated, that he is wanted and needed
and won't be rejected if he fails occasionally. He learns
friendship, sharing, loyalty, the beginnings of service.

In courtship and marriage, the couple enters an ADVANCED
SCHOOL OF LOVE. John and Mary gradually leave "I" and
"you" behind. They begin to think about themselves as "we." As
trust and understanding grow, they become more open to each
other, reveal more of their inner being, and in this very process
of expression, they know themselves more deeply. His vague
thoughts and partially formed dreams become clearer as he
tries to put them into words to order them and test the reaction
of the beloved.

In his wife's loving gaze the husband sees his best self—the one she is recognizing and responding to—a man of strength, nobility and gentleness, the person he could be. In her feminine personality he is inspired to appreciate goodness and virtue itself, as he never understood it in the abstract or never recognized it in a person of the same sex. In her need there are unlocked within him the very things—protection, courage, strength, warmth—that make him a man. In giving herself to him, she has given him to himself in a new and richer way.

The young woman, too, never understands herself as woman until she sees the value her husband places upon her, until she experiences the eagerness, passion, tenderness, reverence and care she can evoke in him. She realizes that for him as woman person she has tremendous attraction and worth. He awakens her to herself as woman.

Spouses who discover themselves as persons in Christian marriage discover much more. As weaknesses and faults are dissolved through confidence, mutual support, courage, communication and joy, each grows in selflessness and dedication. They discover the best of the other as they were conceived in the mind of God and elevated by Christ's redemptive love. They discover Christ's imprint in each other. They stand astonished that God should have made them so and that He should have made them for each other.

Marriage is the advanced school of love par excellence because it provides special circumstances, motivations and challenges that make love grow. There is the mystery and excitement of sexual attractiveness; the delight of psychological intimacy; the security of committed love and partner's responsiveness; the countless opportunities for sharing and serving the other; the leaving behind of fears of loneliness. All of these factors and others, too, facilitate love. They make the hard lesson of dying to self much easier, for in the conjugal process the partners are slowly enticed, challenged and led to forget self and become more and more absorbed in the other until they discover that to love the other as the self is not only possible, but enriching and rewarding. Hopefully, through having experienced the process, they may transfer their experience, their willingness to risk themselves, to their children and all around them.

SACRAMENT TO THE WORLD

To act fully as a sacrament, marriage must begin with a public ceremony, a public commitment. Why? Quite simply because a sacrament is a symbol or sign, and a sign to be effective must be public. You don't paint a NO SMOKING sign and hide it in a closet. A sign must be "out there" where people can respond to its message or else it is useless.

The ceremony must also be public in order that it be a full commitment. If George and Susie marry each other some evening in the front seat of the car by pledging their eternal love and even going through a form with "I do's" and everything, this is still not a full commitment simply because nobody knows about it. Society is unaware of it. If George should change his mind in three months, or if next summer Susie should decide she likes Ralph better, he or she can move out of the private "commitment" and it costs them nothing. The partner more willing to hurt the other can leave the relationship without embarrassment, questions from friends, alimony or even regret. All he has invested is a certain amount of temporary emotion. This is not marriage. This is not sacrament.

"The temporary affair or trial marriage is to real marriage as standing on the high board day-dreaming about what it might be like . . . is to diving."

The public ceremony gives the sacrament its fullness. God's creative love, His unqualified giving without desire of return (for in truth man can add or give nothing to God) is a mystery so profound, paradoxical and foolish that we are baffled before it. When Christ calls us to participate in this totally selfless love, he tells us we will be called foolish.

To help our understanding of divine love, God gave us another living symbol, the Christian married couple. To those who doubt the existence of any true, committed, selfless love, the devotion of husband and wife stand proof of love's reality. To those who fear selfless giving as a demeaning loss of autonomy or dignity, Christian lovers rather testify to the transforming and ennobling power of such love. To men who seek the meaning and fullness of life, the life of the Christian couple proclaims Christ-like love is the essential key to meaning.

FIDELITY AND COMMITMENT

Those who argue against the permanence of marriage say, "Now that people are living so much longer and society is changing so rapidly and radically, it is unrealistic to ask a young man and woman to commit themselves to any institution 'forever.' " One author says any institution that has the failure rate of 1 in 3, as marriage does, ought to be declared illegal.

How can one respond? First by saying that *marriage is not a static commitment to an institution. It is commitment to a person, a process and a vision.* What the vows really say is something like, "I choose you, I accept you as friend, lover, spouse to live an adventure. We agree to support and challenge each other to share our lives in the most intimate ways as we try to grow and become."

The person who cannot foresee the possibility of change in his partner . . . that George, whose prospects are now so bright may never make more than $142.00 a week, or Susan who is a real swinger may soon decide that she rarely wants to leave her home and children; that person may not be ready to pronounce the marriage vows. Change is what it is all about, for marriage is not ultimately based on passion, romance or the static notion of never-ending bliss. It must have its roots in friendship and the willingness to change together.

Man is radically different from Big Bird, Smokey the Bear, or any other animal because he can shape and choose his future. Only man has freedom. Freedom is such a unique and crucial human gift that it would be true to say that "man is freedom." It is part of his deepest self. But man does not truly give himself to another until he gives (gives up) his most unique and precious quality—his freedom. Forsaking all others is a momentous step. But closing off other options is not a negative process. The forsaking should be the by-product of freely and lovingly focusing down on and investing deeply in one other person.

Man is a limited being. He has just so much nervous energy, imagination, attention, concern and intimacy to bestow. If he truly *invests* himself in one other person to live completely in the heart and mind of his spouse and make her growth his destiny—he cannot give himself to others in this fashion. He no longer possesses himself. He has made a gift of himself.

But cannot a man manage a wife and a mistress, or a wife and a succession of affairs, or even perhaps two wives? Yes, he might "manage" such a situation but only by dividing himself, by playing games, by reserving parts of himself and withdrawing from a total love relationship with anyone. The beloved does not merely want to be wanted, but to be prized, cherished, and preferred. The beloved wants to command the unreserved esteem and loyalty of the lover to be viewed as uniquely different and special.

In a "limited liability" relationship ("I love you but I am not closing off other possibilities"), there are whole areas of the self that are not risked or hazarded. The psychic inter-subjectivity and total sharing are stunted because there is a holding back, the guard is up and the defenses are poised and many of the contact points of deep intimacy are blocked.

TIME DIMENSION

In a true marriage the individual's very identity and self-perception becomes basically altered. The other becomes part of the self, part of one's most private psychic life. The sharing that takes place reaches into the very bone and core of each partner's being. They share in the most basic, primitive, intimate events, needs, symbols, rituals which deeply affect personality and create a very unique bonding. They share name, privacy, bed, food, sickness, fear, family ties, secrets, moods, nakedness, disarray, status, economic survival, religious convictions, children, pregnancy, death. They really do become psychically one to a very great extent.

Marriage to be true marriage, to be fully productive of mutual growth must have a future dimension. It must have security and time.

The partners must rest secure in the continuance of each other's love, secure enough to be able to give over some of the defenses and "attraction games" of courtship and honeymoon in order to move on to deeper levels of living. They must be able to walk firmly on the path of deep trust without stepping off into jealousy and anxiety on the one side or complacency and "taking the partner for granted" on the other.

"The fact that Sam not only loves me but that he proves his love by binding himself to me socially, publicly, legally makes me believe that his love is real, that it is important, that I am truly important to him. I can relax, I can move on, I can show more of myself, I can risk more of myself, I can move more deeply into this relationship."

The partners need time to test each other, to correct mistakes, to say "I'm sorry," to taste a wide range of experiences together. They need a future dimension so that plans, reveries, dreams and possibilities can challenge, entice and inspire them. They need the sense of "forever" so that they can construct a future on the sound basis of a firm relationship. Can you conceive of the young lover saying, "Susan, I need you. I want you. The sun rises and sets upon you. I cannot live without you. Will you marry me for a year-and-a-half?" The very idea is grotesque. The deepest thrust of true love implies "forever."

The Christian ideal of marriage says, "forever." For every marriage "in the Lord," bespeaks and shows forth the indissolubility of the bond between Christ and His people.

CONJUGAL SPIRITUALITY

Be spiritual! Who me? Nonsense! That's for cloistered nuns and slightly odd old women who go to evening devotions.

Another confused area. Spirituality basically means being responsive to the promptings of the Holy Spirit of love. In marriage, spirituality doesn't mean you have to undertake old-fashioned or unusual pious practices. Marriage in and of itself is a way of spirituality.

Spirituality in marriage may mean some asceticism and self-discipline, sometimes chosen like cutting down alcohol intake or guarding temper, sometimes accepted like a limited budget or unpleasant relatives. This sort of discipline is good, not in itself, but because it helps us to learn to love more deeply. The man who wants what he wants when he wants it, who is driven to fulfill every flash of impulse that comes into his imagination can never put himself second and truly think of another.

There is a sentence in the old marriage ceremony that says, "Love can make sacrifice easy and perfect love can make it a joy." This is not just double-talk. Consider how much easier it is to do something, even something difficult, for the girl (the boy) you're engaged to than it is to do the very same thing for your annoying brother or sister. Spirituality is loving and then having the understanding and strength to do what love demands.

In marriage, too, spirituality means that you take the trouble to foster an awareness of the Christian dimension of life in your relationship. Maybe you do it with art objects or occasionally going to special liturgies which really "speak to you." Maybe you do it with discussions with your friends, maybe with an adult education class, maybe with ritual in the home starting with Christmas and Easter and working through the other religious events of the year. Maybe you do it by putting aside a few dollars for a decent magazine subscription that talks about the Church and the issues of the world or by buying an occasional paperback that keeps you abreast of the many swirling changes going on in the field of religion. If the Christian dimension is to be kept alive and have some meaning, it must be nourished. You can't get by on what you remember from elementary school.

BEYOND MARRIAGE

Conjugal spirituality means moving beyond the family. Marriage is not enough. Marriage is not the total answer to a mature man or mature woman's needs . . psychological, emotional or spiritual. The couple who says, "We are now married. Our life is fixed. All we need is each other," is in for disappointment. Marriage will not fill all your needs for achievement, interest, involvement, status and opportunities for service.

Marriage is a means. It is an excellent way to live the Christian life and learn the lesson of love. But marriage is not an end. Rather, it is a launching pad that occasionally sends you out, sometimes together, sometimes separately, to greater service in career, the neighborhood, community, world. The family is a nuclear community of love which should reach out and radiate its power to heal, console, inspire and serve all other people.

"Great as the family is, its members can love it too much. It must not become an egoism of two people, exclusive and unconcerned with mankind."

26

> "Love the other as you love yourself."
> "When the security, satisfaction, and development of another become as significant as your own security, satisfaction, and development, then love exists."
>
> Harry Stack Sullivan

What Does Love Look Like?

John Donne said, "No man is an island." No man can exist unto himself alone. Alone and separated man is anxious and fearful, for there is no one to reflect back to him that he is good, desirable, appreciated, or even to notice that he is alive. Life in isolation is sub-human.

LOVE AND LONELINESS

Man seeks to overcome aloneness, perhaps by getting lost in the herd or pretending to belong by conforming and being like everyone else. Sometimes he seeks meaning in feverish, time-consuming activity. Sometimes he tries promiscuous sexuality, hoping that the primitive wound of loneliness in his spirit will be healed by these passing encounters.

To overcome loneliness, a man has to "be for others," to be with others, but not just by having them around physically. He needs to be involved in the consciousness, the spirit, the psychic lives of other people, in their feeling, caring, sharing, suffering, laughing, growing, and even dying.

To be human is to spend a lifetime searching for total fulfillment and happiness. To be human is to thirst for final meaning, as echoed in the words of Augustine: "Our hearts are hungry, Lord, and will never be at peace until we are at home with Thee." To be human is also a movement toward this final goal of being totally known and desired. It is a becoming, a growing into relationships where we are understood, wanted, appreciated, cherished, challenged and secure. Real living is a movement into communion with other people, into inter-subjectivity through which we mingle our lives with others on the deepest levels and grow out of loneliness.

LOVE IS

Love is the outreach of our personality that thrusts us into the heart's concern of another person. Love is our personality seen without masks—caring, responsive, trustful, able to touch and open the other.

"Your slightest look will easily disclose me,
Though I have closed myself as fingers,
You open always petal by petal myself,
As spring opens (touching skillfully,
   mysteriously) her first rose."

Love is the re-focusing of attention away from myself and onto the other.

"Love the other as you do yourself?"
"How do you do that?"
"Well, no matter how angry you get at yourself,
you never stop talking to yourself.
When you do something stupid, you always give
yourself the benefit of the doubt.
Whatever problem or situation confronts you, your
first consideration is always, 'How will it affect myself?'
Well now the trick in loving is to say, 'Self move over.
From now on she (or he) is going to start getting this
special treatment, too.' "

"Love is making a gift of yourself."

LOVING AND GIVING

It is better to give than to receive. Why? Because giving is sometimes difficult and I suffer and feel noble? That's not the real reason. When I give myself in love, it is the highest expression of my power as a person. I know that I am

28

something, I have something, be it time, counsel, tears, a word, an embrace, that is truly valuable because the other needs and desires it. When I become, and am accepted as, a gift of love, the scales fall from my eyes and I recognize myself as valued, worthwhile and good.

In giving, the beloved is enriched. I enhance the other's sense of dignity and personal value by offering the proof of my constant care and concern. If two people truly love each other in this fashion, they discover themselves anew. For love is blind to (makes allowances for) the weaknesses and defects of the other. It shines a light on and activates the best qualities of each and the lovers share a sense of aliveness, a new level of being, which they have brought to birth.

"I love you
Not only for what you are
But for what I am
When I am with you.
I love you
For putting your hand
Into my heaped-up heart

And passing over
All the foolish, weak things
That you cannot help but see there
And for drawing out into the light
All of the beautiful qualities
That no one else had ever looked
Quite far enough to see."

LOVE IS CREATIVE

It creates the lover. If I "love" an orange and eat it up, I gain something—protein, strength, energy. If I "love" a symphony and let its sound flow over me, the thoughts and feelings it inspires become part of me. I am richer for the experience. If I love another person, then I will undergo the deepest transformation. Mirrored in the eyes of the beloved, the lover sees his ideal self.

From Susan, John gets a vision of what she wants him to be, of what she believes him to be, and what he might be. Given the security, inspiration and challenge of her love, he dares to change, to become his best self. He may fear and become more sensitive. He may find the courage to take risks. Or, he may unlock the energy to live up to the talents he possesses. He grows in pursuing the vision of himself which she has revealed.

The beloved is created. The young wife bringing typical strengths, weaknesses and pretenses into a marriage is created in the strong, loving arms of her husband. She says to herself, "Although he knows me intimately, and has seen the worst of me, sometimes bitchy and selfish, yet he desires me. Therefore, even with my defects, I have great value. I am wanted. I am good. I can begin to drop some of my masks and defenses. I don't need them anymore. I can get on with the business of being real."

Married love can draw forth the best of both personalities.

> "Loving people means summoning them forth with the loudest most insistent call;
> It means stirring up in them a mute and hidden being who can't help leaping at the sound of your voice
> A being so new that even those who carried him within didn't know him.
> Yet so authentic that they can't fail to recognize him once they discover him.
> All love includes fatherhood and motherhood.
> To love someone is to create him anew, to bid him to live, to invite him to grow."

ANOTHER DEFINITION

"Love is thinking, willing, and doing the good of another." Neither Smokey the Bear nor Big Bird can really love. Because beyond their limited instincts, they cannot reason to the good of another person. In conjugal love, we are challenged to *figure* out what is *needed* for the growth, development and well-being of the partner. The norm of true love in marriage is not what *I want* for the other and sometimes, not even *what the beloved wants,* but rather what he *needs* to become fully human.

CASE A: (Peter G., Computer Designer—age 31). In six years of marriage gave his wife a ranch house, her own Mustang, a mink and two trips to international Conferences. But he never gave her his time, his thoughts, his heart's concern. His career took too high a priority. He "loved" her according to his will, not her needs. *Result:* Separation.

CASE B: (Margaret K., 27). Her husband is drinking more and more, "because it relaxes me, because I am under pressure, because I know I can handle it." For seven months she watched his social drinking become alcoholic dependency without confrontation. Her norm of love was what her husband wanted, to be left alone, not what he *needed*—help, even if giving it or getting it would be painful to both.

LOVING IS WILLING

The *will* not the emotions is the cornerstone of love. It is possible to love without liking. The beggar who comes to the back door may be repulsive, even frightening. He stirs no positive feeling in us. But if he is met with bread, kind words and some coins, he has been loved.

Warm feelings and deep affection are the ideal mood of a marriage. But strains do come. Paul may sometimes be thoughtless and even cruel. Alice can become despondent and rejecting. It is at these periods when feelings are hurt and hostility wells up, that core love must take over. Stir up the realization that "I am committed to discover, will and do the good of this person even if he is, for a time, unattractive."

This requires certain strengths of personality. The Latin word for strength is "virtus." This brings us to the old-fashioned but really quite important and dynamic idea of "virtue." The best marriages are made by virtuous people, that is, those who are practiced and skilled in generosity, kindness, courage, patience, honesty, etc.

What does virtue have to do with love? Well as light shining through a prism is broken into the colors of the spectrum, so love coming from the personality and encountering concrete life situations (a tired husband, a jealous wife, an irritating mother-in-law, a needy neighbor) is channeled into specific responses, understanding, compassion—which are called virtue.

INNER STRENGTH

A man and a woman schooled in competition and pride cannot simply sit down together and start caring. It takes humility to look wide-eyed at somebody else, to praise, to cherish, to honor.

As Father Capon puts it so insightfully,

> "For as long as it lasts, the first throes of romantic love will usually extort humility from them, but when the initial wonder fades and familiarity begins to hobble biology, it's going to take virtue to bring it off."

This is all obvious in the extreme, but it needs saying loudly and often. *The only available candidates for matrimony are, every last one of them, sinners.* As sinners, they are in a fair way to wreck themselves and anyone else who gets within arm's length of them.

Without virtue, no marriage will make it. Marriage is made of stuff like truthfulness, patience, love and liberality; of prudence, justice, temperance and courage; and of all their adjuncts and circumstances: manners, consideration, fair speech and the ability to keep one's mouth shut and one's heart open, as needed.

SELF-LOVE

"To love your partner you must love yourself first."

Good marriages are made by two reasonably secure, fairly mature, self-accepting people; people who have, and know they have, inner strengths and gifts to bestow on each other. Ideally, *the best marriage prospect is a person who does not have an absolute psychological need to marry,* who is whole enough to make it through life alone.

The worst prospect is the one who says, "I am nothing without you; I can't live without you." If he simply means "I desire you very much" or "I need you to be my best self," that's well and good. But if he really means "I have no inner resources without you; you must fill all my personality needs (and make up for all my disappointments and all the years my mother didn't love me) then he or she may be bringing little more to marriage than a draining dependency."

The person who is always fearful, distrustful, or "guilty," the person who dislikes himself cannot love, because he cannot take the focus off himself. He has not finished his developmental task of discovering his own identity and building his ego strength. Because he is uncomfortable with himself, he is preoccupied with himself. It is rather like the girl who, immediately upon entering the house, knows she "goofed." Her dress is completely inappropriate for this party. She feels awkward and self-conscious all evening. She can never loosen up and get involved in the action.

TO LOVE IS TO RISK

Whenever we trust, we run the risk of being hurt; and as the sociologists say, "significant-intimate" persons can hurt us most of all. People who are important to us and close to us, whose good opinion we need and cherish, a mother, father, husband, wife, child, best friend, can hurt us deeply if they turn on us or fail us.

When such a person is hostile, critical or rejecting, it is a major blow to our ego. First because we have exposed ourselves to this person and count on him as one of the strong supports of our own self-esteem. Secondly, because such negative behavior from someone close is often unexpected and therefore quite shocking and doubly threatening. Finally, an intimate person, especially a husband or a wife, knows us so well that when they criticize, they can "strike to the target," that is, point out our weaknesses and faults quite accurately. They deprive us of the defense of saying, "You don't know what you're talking about."

In marriage you occasionally see each other physically naked but every single day you stand before each other more and more psychologically unclothed. You slowly drop your guard and you reveal your fears, weaknesses and faults. And this is good. For when Tom can say, "Mary knows me as I really am—sometimes messy, often lazy, occasionally frightened—and yet she desires me," this is intoxicating. It is liberating because now he doesn't have to invest so much emotional energy in hiding his faults and playing games. But this mutual revelation can also be hazardous, for as you disclose your weaknesses to each other you put yourselves in each other's power. Tom learns the tenderest spot of all to plunge the knife when he is hurt or angry ("You know, I agree with you. Your nose really is pretty big") and Jane too can pick the most vulnerable area to land her karate chop ("Do you think you'll ever learn to speak English well enough so I won't have to be ashamed of you?").

This kind of wounding can be deadly and damaging. When the partner does slowly show you weaknesses and fears, mark those areas fragile in your mind and no matter how provoked you feel, treat them carefully or you could be pushing the red button for a devastating, atomic war. You will sometimes hurt each other, but one of the great things about marriage is that it provides your love with a time dimension. There are many tomorrows that can be filled with reconciliation and healing. Young love is a leap of faith. Take the risk. Leap bravely and don't look back. Give each other trust, loyalty, confidence, the benefit of a thousand doubts.

LOVE IS RESPECTFUL

"Respect" comes from two Latin words, "re" which means again as in re-turn or re-make and "spicere" as in spectacle or spectator, which means "to look." Respect means to look again, to look more deeply, to look with the mind and the heart, to recognize and appreciate the partner in his own personhood, his own dignity, his own unique share in the human spirit.

You must respect the very "otherness" of your partner and not mold, spindle or manipulate him into the form you desire. Don't dare place your own limited vision of what he or she should be before the destiny God gave him.

Respect means that Tom will help (not just allow) his wife to grow and unfold in her own way, to become the best possible Jane Brown, even if this means encouraging her talent to write, study, weave, or what have you, even at the cost of time she might spend keeping him company. Respect means that Jane will encourage her husband in the talent he has, say, in service projects for the community, even if she prefers that nothing ever draws his interest away from her.

Respect means you don't expect your wife to cook or to pick up your wet towel off the bathroom floor the way your mother did. "Look again, she's not your mother." Respect means you don't expect your husband to treat you like a little girl and make everything nice all the time. He's really not your father.

Respect means you stand a little in awe before the mystery of this person given into your care.

THE OPPOSITE OF LOVE

"The opposite of love is not hatred, it is indifference."

"The opposite of love is not hatred, it is indifference."

The above repetition is not a misprint. It was done to drive home the point. Joe says, "I never want to hurt Mary." Mary says, "I could never hate Joe." They are largely telling the truth. Even after they file for divorce, most couples don't want to hurt each other. They have shared some good years together. They somewhat regret inflicting pain, *but they really just don't care how the other feels.* They are indifferent. They want out, now!

Love in marriage does not die with a bang, but with a whimper. It is usually a process of slow erosion, of boredom, of taking each other for granted, of neglect, of not investing time, attention or imagination in each other.

Enthusiasm leaves first, then concern, then caring, and two people roam around, lost in the husk of an empty marriage. It's easy, then, to see how very soon something or someone else comes to look better and more attractive and now the end is near.

"How do you prevent it?"

Keep alive! Keep growing as a person! Keep bringing your partner the gifts of new ideas and insights, of deeper feelings, of enthusiasm, laughter, new interests.

"If your marriage is not daily being born it is dying."

"Love is a task. Good marriages do not just happen. They are the result of dedication, commitment and effort and effort and effort."

> *"Love is an activity not a passion*
> *Its essence is to 'labor' for someone*
> *To make someone grow*
> *To love a person productively implies*
> *To care and feel responsible*
> *For the development of all his*
> *   human powers."*

"The second hardest thing in all the world is to engage in the trying process of living intimately with one other person.
The hardest thing in all the world is living alone."

"Marriage is a process not a state.
Marriage is a beginning not an end.
Marriage is a threshold not a goal.
Your wedding certificate is a learner's permit not a diploma."

Building Relationship

Several hundred psychology students were each given a piece of colorless paper, told to chew it, and identify the taste. Over 40% said sour, 30% sweet and 20% said bitter. Less than 10% got the right answer. The paper was tasteless. Where did the 90% get the sensation of taste? Why from their imagination, expectancies, and experience. This is a typical example of how we construct reality to suit our views.

I. SEE IT MY WAY

We see everything through the unique lens of our own mind-set and expectancies. Each of us lives in a personal, private world which we carry around with us constantly and call reality. We interpret events, ideas and even people to suit our views. Marriage is the meeting of two such private worlds. These worlds may crash in a head-on collision that shatters both. They may orbit near each other for forty years without ever coming into close contact. Or, they may slowly merge together into one richer world than either could ever be alone.

THE INFLUENCE OF THE PAST

You and your fiance have been conditioned by twenty years of experience. Family, friends, social class, work life, education, the media have molded each of you in a special way. Your personalities have different strong points and weaknesses, different levels of self-confidence, different systems of defense. You have many preferences, convictions and prejudices that are different. Your patterns of learning, decision-making and problem solving vary. Your life styles may be at odds.

The worst possible mistake you can make in a marriage relationship is *to presume that your partner will exactly mirror your attitudes,* ideas, reactions and behavior patterns. HE WON'T! SHE WON'T!

SUSAN AND GEORGE

Susan's father is a little overweight. He drinks too much, but he's always outgoing, affectionate, generous and playful. He sings songs with his children, hugs and pinches his wife even when the kids are around and runs to any neighbor who needs help. George's father, on the other hand, is taciturn, undemonstrative and stern. He will not get involved in anybody's problems, and for him, children ought to shape up or ship out.

It is entirely possible that George and Susan will have quite different sets of expectancies as to what a husband and father ought to be. Unless they understand each other's mindsets, they are in for friction and misunderstanding.

Add a hundred other like situations. Susan has had few opportunities for social contact. She is shy and threatened by people. George has been a back-slapping extrovert since fourth grade. To Susan, Jane Fonda is a heroine, John Wayne a fink. For George, Fonda is a traitor and Wayne a patriot. George believes breakfast is the most important meal of the day and it should be big and hearty. Susan can barely choke down orange juice and a crust of toast before noon . . . See the possibilities?

THE BLENDING BEGINS

"Are not many of these differences resolved during court-ship?" Well, yes and no. Courtship does begin the blending process. You discovered and responded to qualities in each other which you found personally attractive, her liveliness, the way she laughed and could put people at their ease; or, in turn, his seriousness, his drive or even his weird imagination.

You discovered you had many common interests and were indignant about the same issues. As time passed, you talked about the future, compared experiences, dreams, and life goals and found that they fitted together pretty well. As things got more serious, you checked on each other's attitudes toward marriage, money, in-laws, children, life styles and found many levels of agreement, enough to say, "Let's get married."

Won't this blending process begun in courtship simply continue? Hopefully it will, but problems do come. There is truth in the old saying, "You don't really know someone until you live with him."

THE LIMITS OF COURTSHIP

During courtship you had only a *limited range of opportunities to see your fiance in typical life situations,* to discover the attitudes or behavior he or she might display in stress, crisis, boredom or conflict. It is entirely possible you had no chance to see some deeply rooted differences in temperament or expectations, his uncontrolled temper when fatigued and irritated, or, her tendency to call it quits and withdraw when life gets too confused.

During courtship too, both parties are often *on their good behavior,* like the salesman trying to impress a new customer. You both take pains to conceal faults and flaws and project your best, most admirable image.

Again, *new love* with its heady discovery of being wanted and needed, with the excitement born of nearness and the promise of sexual fulfillment turns the lovers gaze away from problem areas. It leads them to discount or minimize any negative traits they might dimly suspect, and to endow the partner with all good qualities: "She's the only girl in the world," or, "He is one in a million."

With marriage your partner does or should become the most intimate, important, ever-present factor in your psychological environment. Questions like, "How would she feel about this?," "Would he approve of that?," become an ingrained part of your thought patterns. This is a major change.

Before marriage you could pretty much act to suit yourself—buy the cocktail dress, take a flyer on the horses, change jobs, tell the boss off, let the car get filthy, sleep all weekend, and blow your savings on a vacation you couldn't afford. If a situation got too sticky or stressful, you could walk away from it. After marriage you are never again really quite that free. It's a different ballgame.

THE NAME OF THE GAME

The name of the game is *adjustment*. It means literally to move towards what is fitting, appropriate, just or necessary for both parties. It is a blending, a meshing, an accommodating, a fitting together of two personalities on every level from sharing the deepest emotions and dreams to the practicalities of maintaining a satisfying family life together.

Adjustment is a game that requires two players. The anecdote of the dominating bride who, upon leaving the chapel with her groom after the ceremony says, "Now that the two of us have become one, let me make it perfectly clear which one it's going to be,"—is a sorry caricature of what adjustment intends and requires.

Adjustment is not submission. Adjustment does not mean tinkering together a life arrangement that is just tolerable, putting up with each other in a sort of cold war. Adjustment is a creative process. It means a full willingness to recognize, accept and promote the unique potential of your partner.

PERSONALITY FIT

Adjustment is the daily and continuing inter-action of two people in love trying to fit their personalities together. Your marriage is a complex mosaic of potential grandeur which you create piece by piece, experience by experience, decision by decision as you confront the intimate, dramatic and routine experiences of your life together.

Notice, we're talking about personality fit and mutual agreement, not right or wrong, or better or worse. If George believes his wife must never use his first name or speak unless spoken to or make any decisions at all, and Susan sincerely believes exactly the same thing, they could have a high degree of "fit" and compatability. They might be reasonably happy, even though a psychologist-onlooker would say George is a dictator, Susan a doormat.

The frequency with which you hear the expression, "I don't know what she could possibly see in him" (or vice versa) is proof that the marriage relationship is unique and highly personal for the very qualities that attract Susan to George or you to your fiance might seem inconsequential, negative or even repulsive to other people.

THE PROCESS

Marital adjustment is the mutual, on-going creative process of *psychological negotiations* (hopefully facilitated by love and respect) to build a relationship that is satisfying to both parties (as individuals and as partners) as they meet and constructively respond to the challenges and decisions of making a life together.

What do these psychological negotiations look like and how are they carried on? Perhaps the process can best be viewed in the area of decision making.

The question: How close shall be the ties we maintain with our in-laws?

a) *First, consider the real issues involved.*

—Our relatives would like us to be close and to visit frequently.

—We do want to keep contact. We have mostly positive feelings toward our families.

—We don't want to get smothered by them and get trapped into visiting patterns they will want to maintain for the next thirty years.

b) *Analyze how you really feel about the issues.*

He: I really don't mind going to her parents' house. The food is good, but after a couple of hours it gets boring as blazes. Or,

—My family is all gone and it's nice to be a part of hers. Or,

—I don't have any family so if I go along with her on this, *she owes me something.*

She: His family is fine, but his mother gets too personal and a little critical and I get angry. He doesn't seem to notice or try to protect me. Or,

—We spend so much time with family that we'll never have a circle of friends of our own.

c) *Share your feelings to the best of your ability.*

Really try to tell your partner your hang-ups, your fears and preferences.

d) *How does your decision fit in with your basic life goals?*

—We respect our parents and it is fitting that we should maintain a relationship. Besides they lent us money and we are grateful. Also, children need grandparents. Or,

—Tom's mother is overly-possessive and he needs to, ought to, wants to loosen that tie because it prevents him from operating maturely.

e) *Consider which of you has most at stake in the decision.*

—Susan is the only daughter of a doting father. George is one of nine children and his parents barely remember his name.

f) *Consider who must live with the decision? Who will take the consequences?*

—Both of you, but Susan is going to get a lot more telephone flack from mother and sisters if you don't visit pretty regularly.

g) *How do your friends, relatives and people you admire usually solve the problem before you?*

Does their approach hold any clues for you?

At this point, having considered and talked over these factors, try to draw some conclusions and set up some guidelines *agreeable to you both.*

—We'll try to keep our schedule of visits flexible.

—We'll occasionally try to do things with our parents and not just sit around searching for conversation.

—We'll see them more, or we'll see them less.

—We'll make no major commitments in this area without checking with each other, etc. etc.

Notice, in adjustment the decision you reach is not nearly as important as the process you go through. The more deeply, logically and democratically you analyze and discuss the matter before you, the more constructive moves will present themselves. Both, having had their say and foreseeing all consequences, will be willing to live with the conclusions.

Will anyone really go through the kind of exercise just outlined? Yes, simply because most of the factors described are consciously or unconsciously involved in every decision making process. But making the factors more explicit, spending more time analyzing your feelings and communicating them to each other are skills that many couples should work to develop.

BLACK & WHITE

But what if a black and white disagreement situation comes up? He wants to change jobs and this will necessitate leaving town. She really doesn't want to move.

Again, get accurate information.
—Consider all the factors and feelings fully and honestly.
—Use the constant norm of the present and future good of both partners and the family.
—Try to figure out constructive ways to handle obstacles and hang-ups ("I just won't know anybody in Oregon").

If, after discussion things still come out pretty even, then maybe the consideration of who has most at stake, he with job satisfaction or she with losing her roots in the community, should be given great weight.

Since there are no majority votes possible with only two of you balloting, one has to compromise to move toward the other to say, "Ok, we'll take a flyer and go." Or, "I'll forget about it for now."

There are three special considerations when it comes to this *moment of truth*. One is the temptation to dig in and stand pat. Perhaps Susan says to herself, "His reasons are sounding more sensible all the time, but if I just keep saying no, I know he will give in." Mistake! If one opinion begins to look better, move toward it. Remember the object of the dialogue is wise decision and good adjustment—*not winning*. Every time there is a winner, there is a loser, and after a while losers get pretty surly.

Secondly, the one who makes the compromise should do so as wholeheartedly and enthusiastically as possible. You are a team. Once the play is called you both exert yourselves to make it work. Don't lie back waiting for a chance to shout, "I told you so."

Finally, the one whose point-of-view prevails should be especially solicitous, supportive and ready to help in the problem areas the other fears.

Cautions

1) Be wary of reaching a "final" decision on your own and then doing all you can to induce or manipulate your partner to accept it. Real dialogue requires that you be open to changing your viewpoint.

2) Try not to think in terms of who's "right" and who's "wrong." There is no moral significance (real rightness or wrongness) about the color of your new car or where you spend a vacation, or, for that matter, about most of the decisions you have to make. The right-wrong distinction tends to lock you into rigid black and white positions. The partner who claims that "right" is on his side, is saying, "You are wrong and therefore bad, inferior, and you ought to feel guilty." Try terms like effective or less effective, more or less mutually satisfying, even more or less sensible in the long run. These terms allow room for maneuver.

Many people think we love each other therefore decisions are easy. Really it goes the other way. We work hard to negotiate good decisions and in the process love grows.

THE GOOD ADJUSTOR

There are several key qualities that help a person in the process of adjustment.

The first is autonomy. This means a certain wholeness of personality and independence of spirit. It includes knowing who you are, what you want and need to make you happy, and the courage to pursue it. The autonomous person has the ability to compromise. He knows what he is doing. He has enough self-confidence not to be threatened by giving in on certain things, for good reasons. He is strong enough to be tender, patient and gentle without fearing he will be called weak.

43

He also knows when not to give in. He won't make a deal like the following: "You don't want me to see my family, all right, have it your way. We'll never go there again." He realizes that resentment and repressed hostility in such a situation might lead him to look for ways to even the score. So, he won't agree to an unrealistic compromise that may "kick back" on both of them. He is willing to take the flack right now and seek a more constructive solution.

Another quality is empathy, the skill of feeling what the other person is feeling. Related ideas might be reading the other's moods, being sensitive to the other, compassion, or having "good antennae."

A wife who can recognize how her husband feels about that neighbor, this expenditure, that visit, this plan, can respond more realistically and constructively to him. If she can pick up more subtle feelings like confusion, anxiety, discomfort, she can tune in very precisely on his moods and views. If, further, she can discern the intensity of his feelings, say either enthusiasm or opposition for some project they disagree on ("Let's have all the relatives over for Easter this year") then she can understand the need for proceeding carefully. Nothing can cause more resentment than interference with or lack of support for a strongly committed position which one partner has taken.

Empathy can be improved simply by practice, by paying attention to clues, by seriously attempting to "track the other's feelings," by asking how the partner felt in certain situations and discerning patterns that will probably hold true in their future.

Next there is creativity. The creative person is the one who is convinced that there is more than one way to skin a cat and is willing to look for it. She has imagination, can figure out options, can brain-storm possibilities, can substitute one solution for another, can go around obstacles and seek alternatives. She doesn't panic when extra guests show up or when her plans have quickly to be changed. Her husband loses a sale and is deeply depressed. She might call his male friends in for a night of poker and complaining about their jobs, rather than feel she always has to do the consoling bit singlehandedly.

44

The creative person is open to new ideas, is stimulated rather than depressed by challenges and is not hung-up on the famous seven last words, "We never did it that way before."

In adjustment negotiations, when confronted with problems like, "We need some extra income; the car won't last another six months; my new boss doesn't appreciate me; how can I tell mother she's spoiling the kids; how shall we decorate the living room; how can we repay our social obligations within our budget," it's a valuable exercise to see how many different solutions you can dream up, no matter how wild and far out. Often you discover possibilities never dreamt of.

Skillful, honest, open communication is such an important factor in adjustment that we have given it a chapter all its own.

ADJUST WHAT

There are scores of areas from the trivial to the vitally important which will require adjustment and decision-making in your marriage. Here we list a few you might not have thought of just to stimulate discussion.

APPEARANCE, especially at home. Will his underwear and bare feet approach offend her? Will her curlers insult him? Do you expect him to shave on a day off? What do you expect?

PRIVACY—You will rarely be alone. Do you need time by yourself to think, reflect and putter? How do you tell your partner without seeming to be rejecting?

SOCIAL LIFE—He says three or four nights a month out alone with his male friends is a minimum. She says we married to be together. What do you say?

ENTERTAINMENT—"The Courtship of Eddie's Sister-in-law" is her favorite program. It makes him retch. Or, he never heard of the National Education T.V. Network, while she can only enjoy a program when she knows it's so highbrow and good for you that nobody else is watching.

HOUSEKEEPING—How "clean" is "clean?" How neat is neat? Where do *you* draw the line between informal, lived-in and sloppy?

PACE—He is a morning person (there are a few) who leaps out of bed and plunges into the day. At sunset he begins to wind down. She gets her second eye open about 2 in the afternoon but can go on half the night. He's a charger. She likes to savor things.

GROWTH DIFFERENTIAL—He is moving up, greater work responsibilities, learning new things, meeting more people, seeing a wider world. She's the same sweet, simple kid he married, still spelling her way through MAD magazine. Or, he has grown in nothing but paunch since their wedding day and is dull, dull, dull; while she takes every adult education course available and joins every movement to make a better world.

RITUAL—For her, things should be done with style and grace. Meals are an occasion, Christmas takes weeks of planning; anniversaries and birthdays are very special; gifts and the words that accompany them carry deep meanings. He is much more matter-of-fact and can't get excited about frills.

II. CHILDREN AND ADJUSTMENT

Marriage is not necessary for begetting children. Over 100,000 babies are born out of wedlock in this country every year. Marriage is necessary and ideally suited for procreation in the fullest sense, the having, raising and forming of children into healthy persons, responsible citizens and committed Christians. *Making babies is not the purpose of marriage.* Parenthood is a biological, psychological, socializing process involving nurture, love, care and time. Marriage is about making persons. The service to new life which you undertake is not accomplished within nine months of pregnancy. It requires the investment of years and decades.

THE ENVELOPE OF LOVE

In pregnancy, the child lives in a perfect environment in his mother's womb. It is perfect as to light, darkness, nourishment, temperature, insulation from shock, etc. When he leaves this in-between world, the child has a right to be born into the best possible human environment, the community of a loving family.

Sociologists tell us that the best possible environment for the

46

rearing of the child is a very small, intimate community where the child has available both a male and female role model, where there is care, nurture and a high degree of continuing mutual commitment so that as he grows, his aggressions can be tolerated, his ego strengths developed and through guidelines and practice he can be "fitted" into the culture in which he must operate. These gentlemen are describing marriage, not from any set of reversible principles, but simply by analyzing the basic needs of a child and how they can best be served.

THE SERVICE OF NEW LIFE

How do you feel about children? I hope you haven't been sold a bill of goods by the professional environmentalists who would like to frighten young people into seeing children as a form of pollution, nor by the swinger mentality that says children tie you down, they don't allow you to squeeze all the gusto out of life that you as a free American so richly deserve. "Don't miss a single experience now," they say, "and perhaps you might be allowed to adopt one child when you're 35 or 40 or some ancient age like that."

Living is making choices. Growing up means wisely choosing certain things over others. But to choose anything definitely, with commitment, means that other options are *not* chosen. They are left behind. Only the immature, the fearful and the neurotic want to do everything and be everything. After the age of 11 or 12, hopefully you realize it's unlikely that you can be a combination of astronaut, fireman, President and cowboy.

In your marriage there may be need to limit the size of your family. There should be concern for environment, population stresses and society as a whole. But your attitude must be balanced. You really don't want to be the oldest living adolescent in your town. "There is a time for all things under the sun" and marriage is a time for new life, for moving toward the maturing depth relationship of parenthood.

CHILDREN ARE A GIFT

A child is the usual, natural means of further perfecting the personalities of the husband and wife. By his utter helplessness, appeal and attractiveness the child leads his parents into new dimensions of love. He calls forth new talents and virtues from them and brings them to higher levels of human awareness, understanding and unselfishness. As the relationship between the married couple grows stronger and more secure, they are ready not merely to gaze at and inter-act with each other, but to turn together to love someone who is outside themselves yet still their very own.

In their common concern for the child, the couple shares dreams and plans, pride and anxiety and ten thousand moments of joy, laughter—yes, and disappointment and tears. As husband and wife set up relationship with their children, they are at the same time weaving stronger bonds of relationship with each other.

YOUR LOVE COMES FIRST

The greatest gift any couple can give their children is a love which is consistent, strong, patient, wise and creative. However, for the couple to do this, they themselves must be fulfilled and mature persons. They must be enjoying a relationship which is alive, vital and filled with mutual support. *A good husband-wife relationship is the best guarantee of healthy parent-child relationships.* The wife who feels neglected or taken for granted could easily look to her children for compensations and become a possessive and smothering mother. The husband who feels his efforts are not appreciated might easily turn some of his hostilities and frustration on the children and simply refuse to invest himself in their lives because "I am too busy. I've got troubles enough. Let their mother take care of them. Etc."

Parental love is unlike marital love and in a sense closer to the selflessness of God's love. In marital love there is always reciprocity or the hope of it. One partner loves the other freely and generously and yet there is the almost sure knowledge that he will be loved in return. *Children will never fully reciprocate the love of their parents.* The mature parent knows, or should know, that the child's destiny is to carry the love he has received into the future, to bestow it upon his own children from generation to generation. One of the most bitter-sweet things about parental love is the realization that *your children live in the house of tomorrow* where you cannot follow.

PREPARING FOR PARENTHOOD

As you read this your wedding is still before you or just recently past and you may not be too concerned with the challenges of parenthood. May we, however, plant three or four seeds for reflection?

The first pregnancy works an essential change in your relationship. You are now three. For most young couples, pregnancy is a source of joy; for some it can be a strain. For some young husbands, having to share his wife's concern with a child unborn or newly born can be a threat. For some young wives, the mystery of new life within her can make her too pre-occupied with herself. Then there is the factor of the unknown in the process of being pregnant and giving birth. Learn about it. Get some books. Read some things *together*. Get sound advice. This can be one of the happiest times in your life if you see it as a great adventure you share together.

Learn about parenthood. Feeding a child and keeping it warm is relatively simple. But the dynamics of child development, the effects society has upon children, the tremendous influence of parental attitudes are not so obvious. Discuss and read, but don't be one-book-parents. Try Erickson, Spock and Ginnot and others in the rich literature that is available. The knowledge and intuitions you brought from your own homes will stand you in good stead, but enhancing these with more learning about the art of parenthood can be very valuable and even necessary in this time of rapid change.

Learning Communication

The saddest marriages are those in which two people become
roommates, bedmates, mealmates but still remain strangers.
These people have children, grandchildren, dogs, cats, cars
and houses. They also have frustrations, neuroses, affairs,
divorces; or they live on the edge of quiet desperation in the
barren wasteland of boredom. They never learn the importance
of openness, honesty and trust in communication. They are
unwilling to take the risk of loving, of letting the partner see
and touch the secret places of their being.

Real communication means self-disclosure. Many of us are
so frantic about maintaining our status and about projecting
just the right image—the one which we hope will be applauded
and admired—that we can easily be frightened away from
self-disclosure and forced back to playing games.

50

After the first burst of loving communication in courtship and early marriage, many couples continue to grow in intimacy throughout the years; but as masks and disguises are stripped away in daily living, some couples become fearful and begin to hold back. They limit communication to certain areas. Instead of telling how they feel, who they are, what they dream of, they talk about weather, television and the price of things. Thus begins the slow descent into mutual boredom.

Real union in marriage is born of a special attitude which is a focusing on, a going out to, a readiness to meet and discover the other, and a willingness to disclose ourselves. Communication is the skill which makes this attitude operational.

Communication is the art of sharing experience. In marriage it is the skill of expressing and receiving each other's insights, ideas and feelings in such a way that greater understanding, acceptance and intimacy result. With good communication, disagreements are minimized and differences recognized, understood and respected. Expectations are blended and common courses of action chosen.

THE WAY I SEE IT

If four people are playing bridge the aces have special meaning for them as the most powerful card in each suit. If two of the people leave and the two remaining switch to gin rummy, the aces take on a new meaning . . . the lowest card in a suit. The card itself did not change—not in shape or color— but the meaning which we human beings give to it was changed by mutual agreement. The problem is, of course, that we do not always give the same meanings to words, symbols, events or ideas. Each man sees the world through the lens of his own individual conditioning and experience and this he calls reality.

Depending on your experiences certain names set off different emotional responses in each of you. Read over the following list and select one or two names which you like and your partner doesn't (or vice versa): Mary Ann, Josephine, Helen, Kim, Elsie, Gertrude, Candy, Susan, Bernice, Emily. Now try to analyze and express your feelings about them, and then to discover what in your history has given these names special negative or positive meanings.

We have each developed our own unique personal reactions, (our own package of meanings), to thousands of words: asparagus, dentist, melody, income tax, nudity, home, dutiful husband, housewife, etc.

Try this example: Tom, unwinding from a tough day, stretches out on the couch and Ann leans down to embrace him. "Hey," he sighs, "tonight I really need to be waited on and babied." Suddenly Ann stiffens! Their intimacy is broken as she quickly walks over to finish setting the table. Tom is startled and inclined to be hurt. But being fairly sensitive, he realizes that her abrupt withdrawal must have been caused by something he said.

After some dialogue and gentle probing, Ann herself was surprised to discover that the word "baby" triggered her strong, negative reaction. This word carried emotions from early childhood experience. At her house, to be babied meant to be treated as useless, helpless, worthless—even messy and smelly. It meant to be rejected as too demanding and too much bother—"Grow up. Don't be a baby." Thus, when her husband whom she wants to admire and look to for strength and support wants to be treated like a baby it upsets her considerably.

TRACK THE FEELINGS

How do we enter into each other's reality view, into his or her world of personal meanings? By developing sensitivity and awareness. If your partner should suddenly stop talking, look hurt, withdraw, or react with undue anger, stop the conversation right then and there. What is happening between you in that existential moment is far more important than the bills, plans or problems you were discussing. Stop and ask, "Listen, something I said caused you a problem." Or, "Look, something here has confused you. Can you talk about it so that we can work our way through it?" This way the booby trap can be defused.

This skill of learning to feel what the other person is feeling is called "empathy," putting yourself in the mind, heart and the frame of reference of the other person. However, before empathy can be developed, the good communicator needs self-insight: an understanding of his own feelings.

KNOW YOURSELF

There are people who go through life with only a general, fuzzy awareness of their own feelings. They rarely reflect on them and if asked directly, "How do you feel?" can at best come up with some statement like—"I'm all right" or "I feel lousy." Such people often see no patterns, no cause and effect relationships in their emotional life. Joan receives an unexpected compliment and is elated for hours but she never relates the compliment and mood. John has a major bill to pay at the end of the week and is really worried about it. He goes through his days surly and snappish, quarreling with everyone, never realizing that his preoccupation and fears about his debt are creating these problems.

If we recognize our feelings, we can work with them. Bill is driving home from work. If he realizes that the sale he lost, the cold clogging his head and the boss's irritation have made him depressed, he can enter the house and wave a signal flag at his wife, "Hey, I'm not feeling all that good tonight." If he is not aware of the mood that has crept up on him, when dinner is late or the noise level gets too high, he may release his angry emotions on wife or children without ever realizing that he is using them as secondary targets.

The person who reflects is also able to distinguish and identify his feelings. He can say, "I'm depressed, puzzled, apprehensive, concerned, frightened, ashamed, tired, irritated," all of which have different meanings. If he always lumps emotions under the catch-all title, "I feel lousy," it's very hard to talk about them clearly and understanding is impeded.

The person with little self-insight has great difficulty in empathizing with others. For we must use our experience of understanding our own emotional patterns in trying to understand how others feel.

Dick comes home late from work and finds Susan very uptight. He could: 1) interpret this as an attack on himself and begin to escalate the conversation into a quarrel; or 2) try to "track her feelings," to discover what caused the negative mood. It may have been a badgering phone call from her mother, some real or fancied insult at the supermarket, or even concern for him because the roads were so slippery and she was worried about his safety. In any case, finding causes helps the couple to deal with the substance of problems, not their symptoms.

ACCEPTANCE AND THREAT

An attitude of warm, non-judgmental acceptance of each other is the most important factor in promoting good communication. You've noticed that some people turn us on. They stimulate us. In their presence we speak easily and well. We sense that they are really listening, that they respect us and care about what we are saying. With them we grow expansive, we reveal some of our deeper feelings and far-out ideas because we know they are not just waiting to shoot us down.

Other people have the opposite effect. They threaten us and cause fear which is the greatest block to communication. In their presence we shrink and contract either because they are barely listening (their attitude saying, "You're stupid or too boring to command my interest") or because they seem poised and ready to criticize and find fault. With such people we harden all our defenses and reveal nothing.

The little boy caught breaking a window says, "I will pay for it, but please don't tell my mother." Why? Because his mother is the most significant status person in his life; and her esteem, her good opinion is tremendously important to him. In marriage, too, the partners become special value persons to each other. The husband cherishes his wife's good opinion and doesn't want to let her see his faults or weaknesses. Similarly the wife doesn't want him to see her mistakes and stupidities. Thus two people in marriage can threaten each other even though they are very much in love.

Examples

A person who is trying to express deep feelings is like a man who wants to go swimming in the spring. He tests the water before he plunges in. He dips in his toe. If it is too cold he will go no farther. He withdraws and gives up. So, too, in communication we test each other for the temperature of the partner's acceptance and warmth.

If John says to Mary, very tentatively, "You know, I'm not all that happy with the job I've got." How would you rate the following responses for acceptance or threat?

A) "You certainly shouldn't be. They're not paying you very much money."

B) "I'm not terribly happy with the things I have to do either."

C) "Don't start that again. We've got too many bills over our heads for you to think about changing jobs."

D) "We all get discouraged once in a while. By the way, what do you want for supper?"

E) "You're troubled by the job situation. Tell me more about it."

Ellen tells Dan: "Say, this nice young man came by selling these magazine subscriptions and - - -." Dan breaks in sarcastically, "Don't tell me you were taken by some door-to-door con man!" Immediately Ellen sees Dan as the lord high executioner passing judgment and may well lie to him about the magazines she's bought. But more importantly, next time it will be harder for her to talk to him.

Bob drank a little too much and was quite loud at a party. On the way home, Susan can pass judgment, "You are a drunken exhibitionist!" in which case all he can do is crawl, apologize or strike back. Or, she can tell her own feelings, "You know, I was kind of embarrassed," in which case he can at least say, "Why?" and communication can proceed. She may find out that he is shy and frightened at meeting new people, and at least they are confronting a problem not a symptom.

PRACTICING ACCEPTANCE

Accusations and abrasiveness can undermine acceptance. There are certain phrases couples use that simply invite hostile responses. We've chosen some commonly used phrases, each of which carries a hidden attack. In the first three instances we'll put down what the hidden message might be. In the ones that follow, you try to express the hidden accusation:

"What's wrong with you now?" (There is always something wrong with you. What is it this time?)

"This is more than I can expect from you, but . . ." (You are really incapable of doing this reasonable, constructive, noble thing; but I'll give you a chance even though I know you'll fail.)

"How many times do I have to ask you . . ." (You are trying to frustrate my wise plans on purpose.)

Now try these:

"Didn't you promise me that you would . . ."

"What's the use of reminding you . . ."

"Where did you ever get the idea that . . ."

"I don't want to complain, but . . ."

NON-VERBAL COMMUNICATION

Much of mankind's communication is non-verbal. In our evolution on this earth, language seems to be a later development while expressive movements of the body go back almost to the beginning. The body does speak, from the obvious leaping with joy or shaking with rage to tensing the muscles when we are apprehensive or relaxing them completely when we are warm, safe and contented. Of the eyes alone we say that they can be piercing, flashing, cold, hooded, twinkling, smoldering, dark as pools or blank and dead.

Non-verbal communication is especially important in marriage. In the intimacy of their relationship, partners can recognize scores of expressions and subtle reactions that pass between them which are imperceptible to anyone else. This private, secret language has a very important bonding function to perform. Here they can exclude all others and "speak" to each other alone.

Because posture, gestures and facial expressions are quite often spontaneous and intense, they tend to send out messages more completely and clearly than the words we super-impose upon them. Non-verbal communication is very honest and sometimes stands in contradiction to the words we speak. We have learned to be careful of what we say—to please people, to fit in, to hide our feelings—but we haven't yet learned to control all the signals our body sends out. If in a quarrel one of the partner's says, "All right, all right, let's do it your way," his words may be conciliatory but his rigid body, clenched fist and set jaw may still be shouting defiance, stubbornness, anger. You still have a way to go to achieve understanding.

TOUCH

Touch is also one of the most primitive and expressive forms of human communication. In some areas of our American culture, especially those shot through with our Puritan, Anglo-Saxon heritage, touch is considered suspect. Touch is for emotional Latins or people like Zorba the Greek who hug each other, dance and "carry on." Some married people might have to get over an upbringing in which they were schooled never to touch. They have to learn or re-learn the value of a healing hand, caressing fingers, a protective arm around the shoulders, the joys of rubbing, nuzzling, cuddling that bespeak care and concern.

One of the interesting aspects of touch relates to sexual intimacy. Some women complain in counselling that only time they are touched lovingly is as a preliminary to sexual intercourse. Their concern seems to be that all the other important messages touching might communicate at other times become neglected. Touch becomes stereotyped, used only to say "I want something" instead of "I care about you."

WATCH YOUR TIMING

The mood and setting of your conversation can help determine whether you have communication or controversy. Stress, fatigue, special worries, expectancies, menstrual tension, a common cold, and alcohol are all factors to be weighed in communication.

If George has just finished the income tax and sits staring despairingly at the form, certain he will be a pauper the rest of his life, this is certainly not the time to say, "We really ought to buy something very special for my Cousin Gussie's wedding. We were very close in grammar school." Problems can often be best discussed when both partners are feeling good.

PLAN TIME TO BE ALONE TOGETHER

Avoid the trap of busyness. Especially later on when work life keeps you separated, when children require so much time, energy and attention, when you have joined everything from the P.T.A. to the local chapter of bird watchers, couples can go through hectic week-after-week without communicating.

You might do something as unheard of as taking a walk. If money permits, an occasional weekend away from the children *can* be most beneficial, especially to the children. The best possible parent-child relationships are achieved by couples who work at deepening and enriching their own relationships.

But be warned that this is often easier to say than to do. A commitment made early in your marriage to the importance of taking time out for each other on a regular basis should be kept high on your future priority lists when children and house painting and lawn all make demands.

TELEVISION

There are occasions when television can bring stimulation, great ideas, culture and entertainment into your home. It can also bring third-rate movies, inane quiz shows and serials designed for retarded ten-year-olds. It is very easy to fall into the habit of sitting in a semi-stupor watching shows you're not really interested in. When this happens the TV set provides couples with "instant, incommunicado." Don't let TV viewing become a dulling, deadening, time-consuming habit in your marriage. On the other hand, selective watching and serious discussions about some of the things you have seen, and enjoyed together can make TV an asset to communication, and broaden the horizons of your world.

AVOID THE SILENT TREATMENT

Have you ever been the victim of the silent treatment?
When the other simply will not respond? When it is impossible
to get through to the partner? How did you feel? Hurt?
Confused? Angry? Rejected? Frustrated? Even frightened and
vengeful?

The silent treatment is so diabolical because it symbolizes
the complete rejection of the partner. What is the prolonged
silence saying? Could it be something like this: "Whatever you
do or say, however you beg or crawl, I don't care. I despise
you, your feelings, your motives, your explanations. Forgiveness
is impossible. You can't touch me. You can't get through to me.
For me—zap—you're disintegrated! You don't exist." The
silent treatment is a complete breakdown, a total psychological
annihilation of the other. The person thus treated can only
run away or try to force his way through the barrier by
escalating from argument to shouting and perhaps to violence.
The silent treatment makes the resolution of problems
impossible and can deal love a crippling blow.

Can silence ever be constructive? Yes. When the parties
involved in a fruitless quarrel are just wearing each other down,
one might say to the other, "Look, let's stop now, think about
this some more and talk about it again tomorrow." This kind
of withdrawal from discussion could be healthy. It could be a
time for calming down, a time for refueling and it can be done
without harm, *if* the withdrawing partner clearly signals that
it's a temporary withdrawal and that it is being done for
their mutual good.

LET THE DEAD BURY THE DEAD

When you argue, don't dig up the distant past. One of the
greatest temptations we face when losing a quarrel is to seek
more ammunition. The greatest storehouse of ammunition is
our memory. "What about 1969 when you promised to come
straight home but stayed at the office party 'til past midnight?"
Keep things current. Talk about how you feel now. Realize
that the difference between a quarrel and a discussion is
quite simply that in the first somebody wants to win and in the
second two people want to reach understanding.

KEEP IT TO YOURSELF

Two people are enough for a good argument. Don't involve in-laws, friends, neighbors. Long after you and your partner have kissed, made up and forgotten what the fight was all about, your mother will still be mad at your husband for what he said to you. It's unrealistic, of course, to say never talk about your marriage to your friends. But there are certain levels of intimacy, certain confidences that you just don't disclose except in emergency situations.

AVOID GUNNY SACKING

George gets home from work forty-five minutes late. Susan "blows her top" displaying an anger reaction out of proportion to his "offense." Susan has been gunny sacking. She is still mad at him from the last movie. She has had occasion for a series of reasonable complaints against George over several months but each time she has suppressed and buried her irritation. (Who knows the reason? Perhaps she doesn't like unpleasant scenes? Maybe she sees herself as strong, noble and always able to bear such things? Maybe she is feeling guilty about things she has done which George hasn't called her on.)

Each time an angry, hostile feeling against George came up she stuffed in into her psychic gunny sack which bulged more and more as she dragged it from day to day. Now one final incident causes it to burst wide open and engulf both of them in a messy situation. George is swamped in the whirlpool of her aggressions. He is confused, threatened, and will soon be angry.

When you have an honest complaint, try to face up to it. Clear it up while it is still minor. The marriage relationship can stand more stress and anger than many couples believe possible, especially if both are wise enough to realize "we are now arguing about some limited topic—budget, relatives, vacation—not about whether we love or hate each other." Occasional confrontations and discussions in depth, even if accompanied by friction and anger can be growth situations which lead to understanding. They are certainly preferable to a prevailing, dangerous, artificial calm that covers over honest feelings.

STOP NAGGING

Nagging means—"to annoy by continual fault-finding, scolding, complaining and urging." The trouble with nagging is that it does not work. After the sixth week of badgering George about the screen door, it should become clear that he does not see the problem the way you do. For him, it either has very little importance, or he is tuning you out because he finds the job distasteful for some unknown reason, or he is ignoring the task because he is feeling ornery about something and wants to annoy you, or the whole thing has some deeper, symbolic meaning to him (like junior executives shouldn't do menial things), which is causing the difficulty.

In any case nagging, which works on the principle of setting up such intense and continual irritation that it will finally overcome resistance, is not terribly constructive. It usually becomes a background noise that the other person pays little attention to. Track the feelings. Try to find out why the problem is there and how it can be overcome or avoided.

Nagging involves criticism and implies inadequacy. The unspoken, underlying comment is something like, "Why is it that you are too stupid to do this simple little thing which I see so clearly as important." Nagging often implies bad will, sloth or irresponsibility and is frequently met with a blocking response.

NOTE ON MARRIAGE COUNSELLING

If it should happen that you and your partner develop real problems of misunderstanding or cannot reach agreement on how to solve some of the situations that confront you, you may need to talk to an outsider. If so, choose a wise and mature person or seek qualified professional help. If at all possible do so before the situation gets desperate. Just as travellers in strange lands need guides to teach them the language, customs and geography of the country, so too, some couples get confused or lost in the complexities of the marriage relationship. They need skilled help to understand the terrain and find their way to each other again.

"The most serious danger to a true sexual renaissance in our time comes from the culture's alienation of sex from love, emotion, and commitment. But the resiliency and good sense of mankind may yet prevail. Along with eroticism, the ideals of romance, meaning, fidelity, and love are staging a comeback. Tender concern and responsibility could flourish, the playboy may yet become a man, and the playmate a valiant woman."

Sexuality and Marriage

Sex is not something you do. Sex is something you are. Sexuality, masculinity or femininity, is a basic component of personhood. It is a quality that flows through, informs and shapes your entire personality. *You are a sexed person.* There are no other kinds. Your sexuality is your way of being to the world. You see, react to and judge the world as a man or a woman. The world recognizes and treats you as male or female.

I. SEX IS COMPLEX

Human sexuality has many dimensions. At the instant of conception your bio-chemical structure, your body shape and organs were forever determined. Today any single cell in your body, from hair to toenail, could be sent to a laboratory across the world and the technician there could, upon analysis, immediately say, "This is a male. This is a female." This endowment which you received from the genes of your parents is *sex as gender.*

From the moment of your birth, you were taught sex as *role*. The attitudes of parents and elders, the playthings you were given, the clothes provided you, the chores demanded of you, the games you were supposed to master, the instructions addressed to you ("Little boys are not supposed to cry. Little girls must not play rough") all taught you sex role, the accepted behavior patterns for your society.

Sex is a psychological dynamism. It is a kind of emotional current that flows continuously between boys and girls and men and women. It will remain a part of you and of your personal relationships until about ten minutes after you're dead. In varying circumstances this emotional current can be awareness of difference, interest, excitement, attraction, deep desire or a wanting to be noticed and appreciated by the opposite sex. At times it can be very low key and hardly noticeable, at other times, as in infatuation or first love, it can become surprisingly intense.

Sex is physical intimacy, from hesitant touches and kisses to the total involvement of intercourse. These intimacies are designed for and have the potential of expressing and sharing deep love and pleasure. True, human sexual relations exist in a time dimension. They are preceded by the building of a strong, emotional bond based on deep trust, mutual responsibility and commitment. They lead people to marriage. They heighten, dramatize and cement the already existing bond of love. However, physical intimacies can exist without any significant psychological or love dimension. They can be superficial and next to meaningless or even be a form of exploitation and selfishness.

Sex is communication. Sex is a powerful and symbolic language that reinforces the marriage relationship. The embrace of intercourse can carry many deep messages. The husband can say, "I need you," or, a wife can say, "Even though you failed, I still love you." But these messages confirmed in the marriage bed, are far more total and convincing.

Sex is procreative. Fully human sexuality involves the possibility of and responsibility to new life. The design of the sexual organs themselves, their "incompleteness," the physiology of reproduction and the powerful force that is found in the sex drive all tell us very clearly that one of the chief reasons for sexuality is parenthood, new life and the continuing of the race of man.

"Male and female He created them." The meanings and implications of this mysterious polarity, this division of the human race into two sexes has been pondered, and wondered at by poets, theologians, scientists through the ages and no one yet has explained it fully and completely. *Sexuality is a complex attribute of every person involving his deepest needs for identity, relationship, love and immortality.*

SEX AND MEANINGS

Man puts meanings into sexual relations. He can use sexuality in a hundred different ways to carry many complex meanings. He can involve himself in sexual activity playfully, solemnly, passionately, joyfully, dutifully, or abstractedly. He can use sex to support, to console, to communicate, to seduce, to give pleasure, to share pleasure, to express love and to bond a relationship. He can use it selfishly, to relieve tension, to bargain, to dominate, to punish, insult and exploit.

Sex relations call forth the deepest emotions and most primitive responses of both partners. They involve the most intimate of actions and a very high degree of personal psychological exposure. They require trust, care, openness, a willingness to be vulnerable to this other person, and a concern for each other. They involve a future dimension both with the possibility of procreation and, with the desire to repeat the activity in order to seek deeper communication, meaning and pleasure from it. *Sex relations are uniquely designed to foster the deepest of interpersonal relationships.*

Like sky-diving, motherhood or being drafted, *sex is a definitive experience.* It involves you to the core of your being. You are never quite the same afterwards. Each person who enters sex relations seriously and in a human manner is changed by them. Each forever remains a part of the other. You touch each other at a level of great intimacy with a rich mutual investment of your emotions and psychic life. You are irrevocably enmeshing a portion of yourself with the other.

YOU AND SEX RIGHT NOW

Your attitudes towards sexuality, today, this minute, will have great influence on your sexual adjustment and happiness in marriage. As you are about to take off down the runway, excuse me, down the aisle, here is a flight-check of key ideas about sexuality. You might want to consider them and see how you react.

1. *Sex (even in marriage) was for many centuries thought of as evil, and many people still conceive it so today.*

The reasons for this attitude were many. Women were considered second class human beings, sometimes even objects and chattel to be bartered and used. They were "a source of temptation." The possibility of a deep love, or a friendship relationship with them was not often seriously considered.

Certain dualistic religious beliefs held that there were two gods, one of good and one of evil—one of light and one of darkness. All matter, the bodies of men and anything that related to them, were under the dominion of the god of evil.

Mankind knew so very little about sex and reproduction that the whole process was filled with mystery and carried many of his deepest fears and apprehensions.

Experientially man knew that certain forms of sexual misbehavior could lead him to harm himself and others.

Finally, anything that involved pleasure was, during some periods of Western history, considered suspect. This was the result of a theology that focused on certain wrong emphases which held that only suffering and pain were holy. Even though Popes and theologians, philosophers and scientists have taught the goodness of sexuality for decades, sex is still a shadow in the bedroom for many people.

2. *Sex is good.*

God created the body and all it parts. God created human sexuality. He is the author of the powerful drive that leads a young man and young woman to attract each other, to choose each other and to come together in marriage. He made them capable of giving and enjoying pleasure as they express their love in sexual union.

God's gift is good. Like wine and clean air, the eyes, imagination or speech, our sexual powers and our sexual organs are good. Like wine, the eyes, imagination and speech, they can be misused. When used carelessly, superficially, exploitively or selfishly, sex can be sinful.

Sometimes the question is asked, "How can something bad like sexual activity be made good by the wedding ceremony?" That's really a false and stupid question. Sexuality is important, sacred and good throughout a person's life.

Before marriage sex is surrounded by cautions and safeguards precisely because it is so good,—so vitally important to individuals, couples and relationships. Because it is such a strong drive it can lead men to harm themselves and others. Laws and ideals limiting the use of sex before marriage have the purpose of focusing and channelling its proper use as an integral part of a human relationship of committed love.

The twelve-year-old piano student might be encouraged by doting parents to give tinny and boring little recitals to anyone who will listen. In the process the child might come to believe that he really knows something about music and is beyond the need of the serious discipline of study and practice. He is thereby kept from ever learning what real music might be. The young person who gets sexually involved too soon or too often could easily develop the attitude that the chase and conquest of another, the excitement, "kicks" and physical performance are really what sex is about. Thereby he prevents himself from ever discovering true sex with its rich love dimension.

3. *Sex has an important moral dimension.*

Today there is abroad in the land the mistaken notion that sexual activity between any two people who are willing is quite acceptable regardless of commitment or marriage. This attitude is not your personal problem, but the propagandists for everything from Playboy promiscuity, to wife swapping, to "sex in common" communes, sometimes make us feel uneasy with what seems to be their logic and sophistication. Where are they off base?

First, they are over-reacting to puritan-Victorian attitudes of the past. As the pendulum swings from sex as "hush-hush," they would like to move it all the way over to sex as "highest value." For some sexual activity is a combination of ecstasy, therapy, salvation and inalienable right.

There are others who feel that sex is "no big deal," that it is a nice friendly act that's more exciting than shaking hands, but has little more significance. These are the people who, as one writer puts it, may cause the "Death of Sex" by emptying it of awe and mystery, making it common as breathing and incapable of carrying deep meanings.

There is a principle of philosophy which says *"No one can be ashamed of anything unless he also reverences something,"* or again, "Man will feel no shame or pain about his actions or failures in any area unless he values a personal ideal in that area." Thus, accuse a woman of being a "lousy auto mechanic" and she couldn't care less. She doesn't see or value herself as one. Accuse her of being "a terrible mother, possessive, and domineering," and you have a fight on your hands. This is an image she values. Similarly, each man has an ideal of himself as person. From revelation, from the best of humanist thought in our culture, he has an image (clear or confused, conscious or subconscious) of what he could be: generous, noble, just, competent, disciplined, responsible, dedicated, achieving, loving, admirable, even heroic.

Now, alongside this, given his knowledge of the sex drive with its powerful urge toward personal pleasure, toward copulation, toward attracting, possessing and displaying another person,—he realizes that a pre-occupation with sexuality, or a misuse of his powers in this area leads him to deviate from his ideal self and fall short of what he could be . . . and this causes shame.

Sex can lead him to neglect work and career, to use and exploit other people, to deceive himself and others,— ("Honest, baby, this is an authentic relationship."), to separate sex from love and use it superficially and selfishly, to forget other responsibilities, to leave wife and family, to break commitments, etc., etc.

Thus, sex does contain within it the real possibility of harming self and others,—the possibility of sin. But, notice, the evil is not in the body or the organs or in sexual activity itself, it is in separating them from other important values like love, commitment, marriage, family and responsibility.

In a sense, sex is not like liquor or drugs—external challenges which we can enjoy or abuse or *simply ignore*. Sex is a basic internal dynamic that cannot be ignored. It must be confronted and finally either repressed, or channeled and focused in accordance with one's life values, or given completely free rein. Every person must confront and come to terms with his or her sexuality.

4. Feelings and attitudes are more important than techniques.

Preoccupation with detailed and intricate techniques of intercourse is not only unnecessary to successful marital adjustment but can be worse than useless if it leads to a mechanical, problem-solving approach to what is essentially an expression of feelings and human love. This emphasis on technique is similar to the fallacy abroad in some teachers colleges. The curriculum provides the teachers with every tool and method of communication, discussion leading, group dynamics, etc., but often gives them no content, nothing to teach. Similarly, two highly accomplished sex technicians may have nothing to express to each other and their empty performances soon begin to pale.

Human love-making is not a blind, animal instinct. Men and women must think about how and with whom to create love. A basic knowledge of the anatomy, physiology and psychology of sexuality and reproduction is good and necessary, but many manuals carry the matter to a level of gross exaggeration. Their underlying idea seems to be that the amount of sensual pleasure than can be produced is the most important element in sexual relations, consequently every possible source of excitation is constantly to be explored.

Love-making in marriage is just that—expressing love. Anyone who thinks he can long substitute peculiar mechanical skills for real feelings is deluded and headed for disappointment.

5. *The average young adult male does not know "all there is to know" about sex, and there is no reason why he should.*

For too long, knowing all about sex has been equated with "real masculinity."

Two negative consequences flow from this myth. One is that many men really begin to believe they know "all there is to know about sex" and stop learning or trying to learn how to be a satisfying lover to this particular wife, especially in the more nuanced or subtle areas that have to do with the variety of psychological moods, emotions and deeper meanings.

The second negative consequence is that some men resent their wives making any requests, or suggestions, about the sexual areas of marriage. This is too great a threat to his masculine self-image.

6. *Sex becomes boring for a surprising number of couples.*

The nineteen-year-old bride of ten months complains, "Before marriage all he seemed to be interested in was trying to get sex, now he spends more time with his car than he does with me." A twenty-two-year-old husband married two years says, "Sex is routine now. In the beginning it was pretty exciting, even exhil'rating. Now it's just the same old stuff."

How can this happen to young people so quickly? Well part of the blame must be accepted by a society that failed to teach them how complex and profound this area of life is. It focused them too exclusively on physical sexuality. There are some whose early sex experiences are sensuous and intoxicating, but superficial and shallow, because they compartmentalize sex away from feelings, commitment, sacrifice, and interpersonal love. Isolated sex soon turns to frustration.

The people who get into this bind have usually absorbed a whole package of questionable ideas from our society. Pre-marital experiences are not only normal, but necessary. Any form of continence or control is medieval, unnatural, impossible and unAmerican. They often think of the sex partner as playmate or plaything to be put away as a child puts away his teddy bear until he wants to play again. The child feels no responsibility to his blocks, these are simply things he uses for his pleasure and then ignores.

7. There are significant masculine-feminine differences in attitude and response to love-making.

The young man especially is endowed with more rapid physiological reactions and is more easily and deeply aroused by even mild stimuli of sight, sound, and touch and more quickly readied for the whole series of sexual responses. Generally, women are thought to be less likely to be stimulated by what they see, or hear, or read, although they are mostly quite responsive to touch and physical contact.

These observations are broad generalizations. Individual men and women can and do differ very greatly. In love-making as in everything else, it is foolish to say "All men are like this, all women are like that." It is important for young couples to *learn the other partner* and not to assume blithely that she fits neatly into a preconceived pattern of what women are like, or that "his reactions are just like mine" or to be puzzled and surprised, if she doesn't respond to "what I consider to be very stimulating." In many marriages sometimes one partner, sometimes the other, will be the more active or the more passive. Either husband or wife should feel free to take the initial steps leading to marital relations. It is entirely likely, and entirely proper, that the girl will sometimes be the wooer.

II. THE PHYSIOLOGY OF SEX

The physiology of sexuality is well and widely known these days. However, a review can be useful.

At approximately the age of 11 or 12 the young girl enters an important developmental stage called *puberty.* The pituitary gland in her brain sends forth special hormones which cause a period of rapid growth and maturation.

Important changes take place in her reproductive system; that is in the *ovaries,* which produce egg cells, the *oviducts* (or *fallopian tubes*) which carry the egg cell to the *uterus* (or *womb*) and the vagina, a passage from the uterus to an opening between her legs.

OVARIES AND WOMB

The ovaries are two organs about the size of walnuts, located on each side of the abdominal cavity about six inches below the waist. They contain thousands of microscopic egg cells which have been present in the girl's body since she was born. Each egg cell contains twenty-three chromosomes which will complement the twenty-three chromosomes of the male sperm cell to give the baby its genetic code and inherited characteristics.

At puberty *ovulation* begins. Each ovary, in turn, first one side then the other, brings an egg cell to maturity approximately every 28 days and releases it into the fallopian tube. This process will go on for more than thirty years.

The mature egg cell travels through the fallopian tube, a passageway which leads to the top of the womb or uterus. It will take the egg several days to make this passage. If conception, the meeting of a sperm and egg, is to take place, it will almost invariably happen while the egg is in this tube.

The uterus or womb is shaped something like a hollow pear with the open narrow end pointing downward. It is composed of strong, elastic muscle tissue capable of stretching considerably during pregnancy. Every month or so as a mature egg is released from the ovary, hormones activate the uterus to prepare itself to receive and nourish a fertilized egg. The uterus does this by developing a thick, soft, spongy lining. The fertilized egg, containing all the elements of new life and already multiplying very rapidly in size, embeds itself in the lining of the uterus. Here, in this highly protected environment the newly conceived embryo grows and develops through nine months of pregnancy until ready for birth.

The lower end of the uterus is connected to a passage called the vagina which ends in an opening between the woman's legs. The opening is covered over by two folds of flesh called the *labia*. The vagina is the passage which receives the male sex organ, the penis, in the act of intercourse. It is capable of great expansion, for it is also the birth canal, the passage through which the fully developed infant moves from the womb in the process of labor and birth.

MENSTRUATION

Most frequently the egg cell which reaches the uterus is unfertilized and simply dissolves in the fluids of the body. The soft lining of the uterus and the blood supply it contains also dissolve shortly after ovulation and some days later pass out of the body through the vagina in the *menstrual flow*.

Ovulation and menstruation do not take place during pregnancy because hormones sent out after conception or fertilization has taken place inhibit both these processes. (It is an artificial form of these hormones, notably progesterone, that is used in "the pill" to prevent ovulation.) Normal menstruation and ovulation will continue in the average woman until she is in her middle to late forties. They will cease at a time called *menopause*, after which she is no longer capable of bearing children.

THE MALE SYSTEM

A boy enters puberty approximately 15 months after the girl, around the age of 12 or 13. At this time the male reproductive system, which consists chiefly of two organs, the *testicles* and the *penis* is activated.

The testicles are the sperm producing organs in the man. There are two of them and they are about the size of large olives. The testicles are carried in the scrotum, a soft, sack-like pouch, which hangs down between the legs of the man toward the front of his body. At puberty, the testicles begin to manufacture the male reproductive cells called *sperm*. They produce literally millions of them. Each tiny sperm cell has an oval-shaped head or nucleus, and a tail which allows it to swim through the fluids of the body.

The chief male reproductive organ is the penis. The penis, with the scrotum and the testicles are called the male *genitals*. The penis is a fleshy tube-like organ, again located between the man's legs in front of the scrotum. Most of the time it is small, soft and flexible. The tip of the penis, called the *glans*, contains a great many nerve endings and is highly sensitive to stimulation. When a boy is born the glans is covered with a circle of skin which subsequently may have been removed in a simple operation called circumcision.

When the male is sexually aroused, the penis, which is composed of spongy tissue, fills with blood and becomes much longer, wider and very firm. This enlarging process is called *erection*. It is only in this erect condition that the penis of the man can be inserted into the vagina of the woman.

As stimulation continues, sperm move through a passage from the *epididymis* (where the testicles have stored it) up toward the penis. Several glands add secretions to the sperm as it travels and it is now in the form of a milky-white substance called *seminal fluid* ready to move through a passage in the center of the penis called the *urethra*.

When, in intercourse, stimulation or nervous excitement reaches a peak or climax, the penis goes through a series of rhythmic contractions and, in short spurts, sends forth the sperm into the body of the woman. This process is called *ejaculation*. Shortly after it takes place, the blood leaves the erectile tissue of the penis and it resumes its normal size and softness.

In an ejaculation millions of sperm are deposited in the vagina of the woman. They travel (literally swim) through the uterus and into the fallopian tubes. If they meet an egg cell, one sperm, and only one, will penetrate it and with the mingling of the nuclei of the sperm and egg cells, fertilization or conception takes place and a new life begins.

III. SEX IN MARRIAGE

Couples in love yearn for unity and oneness. They exchange gifts, symbolically trying to give the beloved something of themselves. As they explore each other's personalities, they are delighted to find the same thought in the partner's mind, the same experience in the other's memory. As "I" and "You" become "We," the couple progress to the physical expression of affection. The nearness, the touch, the embrace, kisses, caresses all lead to greater knowing and appreciation.

These expressions of love, significant in themselves, are also a process of preparing the mind, feelings and body for the total intimacy of physical love-making. In the Old Testament, the word "knowing," as in "Adam knew his wife," is a synonym for marital intercourse telling us that love is not just physical but it is the total inter-penetration of two persons.

What follows are human, Christian, realistic suggestions on the beginnings and the growth of sexual love in marriage.

STIMULATION

Certain areas of the bodies of both men and women are especially responsive to sexual stimulation. The mouth, lips and genital organs of both plus the breasts of the woman are the chief sensitive or "erogenous" zones. Beyond that people and moods vary. For some the ears, neck, shoulders, back and thighs, etc. may be highly sensitive areas.

As the couple becomes involved, stimulation of these areas by caressing, fondling, kissing and other forms of contact produces a gradually stronger physical and emotional arousal. There is an increase of excitement and sexual tension and a more intense concentration on the love-making process. At this stage of preliminary stimulation, sometimes called foreplay, there are no right or wrong touches or forbidden body areas. What is desired by one partner and pleasurable to the other is perfectly in order.

In his approach to his wife, the husband ought to display a combination of passion and consideration. With sensitivity and tenderness, he should have due concern for promoting her mounting pleasure and excitement, for avoiding haste and self-centeredness. This is not always easy since many young men are goal-oriented, produce the report, finish the project, make the sale, meet the deadline.

In sex relations, the young husband must learn not to be too goal-oriented, that is, he must enjoy the trip—the by-play, the prolongation of love-making, and not concentrate too determinedly on achieving the orgasm goal. Getting there can be more than half the fun.

Though it occasionally will happen, that one partner participates for the sake of the other's desire in a non-passionate, although affectionate, act of intercourse, the lack of mutual involvement can blight the couple's sense of unity. A monologue with a passive listener, even a loving one, is a poor substitute for an animated conversation. One partner may display a sacrificial accommodation that can be depressing to the other and perhaps leave the "sacrificer" with a feeling of being used. "Thou shalt not be tepid" is a basic marital commandment. In married sexuality, detachment can represent a failure in charity.

THE MOOD OF LOVE

Mood and setting are important. Romantic words of affection and appreciation, dress, the time of the day, the ability to take time and proceed in an unhurried manner, music, the room itself, all provide a special aura of security, well-being, and stimulation that can be of great assistance to your mutual enjoyment of each other.

These "environment" factors are sometimes more important to the wife than the husband. They are part of a "love-arousal" pattern that she appreciates and enjoys. Both of you must check out your expectancies in these matters after marriage. For if a pattern becomes too fixed and repetitious, it can become routine and dull. Some flexibility in time, place, mood, approach and circumstances can also be most agreeable to both partners.

The young wife must be trusting and cooperative, ready to let her love overflow into new emotions and experiences. She must realize that she is capable of a real depth of physical response and involvement. She must not be startled by the fervor of her husband's approach nor yet by the warmth of her own response or by her desire to take initiatives in kisses, touches and caresses to move the process along. The old myth of woman's role as passive is dead. It is also entirely proper for her to make advances and suggestions to begin the activities of love-making without feeling she is bold or forward.

In love-making, nudity is, of course, natural and normal. What form bodily exposure will take—matter-of-fact, seductive, playful—is entirely up to the couple and whatever form it takes is chaste and good. If chastity is defined as "the reasonable use our sexual powers according to the goals of our state in life," then quite obviously, chastity for the married implies full human involvement in the physical expression of love. The conduct of a young husband or wife may be very free, most intimate, playful, passionate and still most chaste.

The visual element in sexual stimulation is quite important, again perhaps more to the man than to the woman. Appearance, dress, the gradual disclosure of the body, postures, positions, are all part of the human approach to sexual fulfillment.

THE PHYSICAL CHANGES

As love-making progresses, definite physical changes occur in the sexual organs of each partner. The entrance to the wife's vagina is covered by two folds of flesh called labia. As stimulation proceeds, this area swells, becomes firmer and somewhat open. At the same time, secretions flow into the vagina serving to lubricate the passage and make it easier for the penis to enter.

The husband's penis becomes firm, enlarged and moist in order to be capable of entrance and penetration. Thus a somewhat similar process of erection has taken place in both partners. As the physical changes occur, not only the woman's body but her emotions, too, are readied. She is open, prepared and eager to receive her husband just as the man's whole being is expressed through his body and is concentrated and focused, ready to give himself to his wife.

THE CURVE OF EXCITATION

As arousal becomes more intense, the entire nervous system becomes involved and ready for the final act of union. Sexual arousal tends to follow a normal curve of excitation which develops at a different rate in different people and usually progresses more rapidly in the young husband than in the wife. It is possible that at this stage, a certain restraint and a slowing down on the part of the husband until his wife is totally involved and ready may be required.

Love-making requires time. If undue haste is avoided and sufficient attention is given to preparatory acts of stimulation, the satisfaction level of both partners will be greater.

In the later stages of stimulation it is useful to call attention to a tiny organ called the clitoris, located within the labia near their upper end. It is one of the most important centers of sexual sensitivity in the woman and it is desirable to give it sufficient stimulation during the final stages preceding intercourse.

Throughout the process of arousal, communication between the couple is important. This does not mean that one partner necessarily gives the other detailed instruction; but acknowledgments in words or sounds that certain actions are pleasing or desirable or are to be continued have the effect of reassuring both partners that things are progressing well. These very sounds of response and appreciation act as further forms of psychological stimulation.

THE CLIMAX

When sexual stimulation is quite intense and both partners feel ready, the penis is inserted into the vagina. Usually it is helpful if the wife guides the husband in this movement. The husband initiates a series of rhythmic, thrusting motions which both partners can then engage in. These movements cause physical and emotional tension to build to a point of climax at which moment nervous tension is suddenly released in orgasm. At this time seminal fluid from the husband's penis is ejaculated and deposited in the vagina of the wife. This swift release of tension is the time of highest excitement and greatest pleasure in the sexual union. It is followed by slow relaxation and a deep feeling of well-being.

Orgasm occurs consistently in the husband. It is always definite and obvious and associated with the moment of ejaculation. Once the process of orgasm begins in the male it continues automatically and it is largely beyond his control to cause it to stop or subside.

The pattern of orgasm among women is more varied. The same wife may experience different responses at different times—sometimes quite marked, intense and evident, with muscular spasms in the pelvic region, sometimes less intense and perceptible. For the wife, orgasm is not always so clear, definite or localized an experience as it is for her husband. It may sometimes be a far more diffuse and less obvious reaction, a sense of relaxation, well-being, of intimate union and satisfaction.

Studies indicate that for many wives a marked orgasm is infrequent in the earliest days of marriage and may not take place until after several months of experience. Again, the fact that the young wife has achieved an intense orgasm is no assurance that her response on all subsequent occasions will be similar. The levels of response will differ depending on time, mood, emotional involvement, physical well-being and other circumstances.

The average young husband usually reaches orgasm quite soon after intromission (the time will lengthen with experience). This may mean that his wife will often not achieve orgasm at the same time. A given act of intercourse will not automatically produce simultaneous orgasm in both partners. Husband and wife must learn through patience and experience the amount of preparatory stimulation that each requires in order to achieve the deep physical and emotional release of which they are both capable. As experience grows, the timing necessary in order to come to climax together will become easier to control.

A word of caution—be wary of writings (even these writings) that hold forth some "ideal" of consistently intense excitement and simultaneous orgasm that is often unrealistic. Further, the fairly recent extensive discussion and publicity given to feminine orgasm in the media may have already resulted in some over-emphasis on achieving this one criterion of sexual success. The female orgasm has for some become a "status symbol" creating anxiety on the part of the man (Can he provoke it?) and of the woman (Can she produce it?). The thought that there is always something "beyond this" that we ought to be experiencing and that we are somehow falling short in our love-making can disturb some couples and create anxieties that may in fact inhibit the process of sexual enjoyment.

POSITION

Some marriage manuals give long descriptions of the positions of intercourse. These are hardly necessary. For any couple with positive attitudes toward sex and real consideration for each other will soon discover the various positions most satisfying to both at different times and under differing circumstances. The husband above the wife is the most common position. The other basic positions—side-by-side, woman above the man and rear entry into the vagina of the woman—are less used but certainly acceptable if they serve the purpose of a human expression of mutual love.

Husbands must strive to remember that the countless love acts— gift giving, careful listening, psychological support, helping with chores, planning surprises, compliments on appearance and attributes—all speak to the wife telling her she is appreciated, preferred to others, desirable, needed and wanted. This love attitude flows over into sexual relations making them more human, warm, personal and fulfilling.

Wives must realize, that contrary to myths about the "physical" nature of the male, the area in the male body that needs most constant stimulation is his mind, his imagination. She must tell him, verbally and non-verbally, that he is attractive, appreciated, wanted and needed spiritually, psychologically and physically. The wife who presumes her husband doesn't require encouragement and reassurance, "and certainly not on the physical level," is usually making a mistake.

Sex relations are one of humanity's deepest forms of communication. "The body speaks most eloquently to tell the love of mind and heart." As you live the years together sharing elation and frustration, setbacks and satisfactions, as you stockpile experiences, and cherished memories you have more to say to each other and this will flow over and shape your love-making. They must not fear temporary abstinence, for as silence is to speech—underlining, dramatizing and giving emphasis to the words spoken—so abstinence can kindle desire, warm the imagination and give deeper meaning to sex relations.

EARLY EXPERIENCES

In the newness and excitement of love-making the young husband sometimes experiences ejaculation before bodily union is accomplished. Such an occurrence is not at all unusual and should not cause surprise, embarrassment or anxiety. If premature ejaculation should occur, the husband will want to delay further love-making for a time (which may vary from minutes to several hours), until the arousal process takes place in him again. As marital intimacies become more familiar, extreme sensitivity will decrease and the problem of premature ejaculation will soon solve itself.

For women orgasm is a more complex phenomenon that can include several stages of involvement and response. Thus young brides may under stimulation experience some level of orgasm before intromission takes place or more rarely she may experience multiple orgasms during the period of sexual relations. Both these occurrences are normal and the couple can and should simply proceed as they desire.

One of the factors that used to cause concern regarding the wedding night was the opening of the hymen. In the young woman the external opening of the vaginal passage is partially covered by a very thin membrane called the hymen. In these days of great activity for women, the hymen is very frequently stretched and opened long before marriage. The condition of the hymen is NO indication of virginity or non-virginity.

If the membrane is intact, it will be stretched and opened during initial sexual union. This occurrence will be felt as a pressure when the male organ is placed in the vaginal opening. As the membrane stretches or opens, a cessation of tension is the only sensation felt by most women. Minor discomfort and slight bleeding may sometimes occur but this should not be the cause of any anxiety.

The fear of pain which a few brides carry into marriage is unfounded. In fact, this fear may be the cause of some pain since it might cause muscular tension making intercourse more difficult. Only in the rarest of cases is it found that the hymenal membrane is so thick that relations are difficult. In this rare instance, a physician should be consulted.

In this context a little sensible planning about the wedding night and honeymoon can be useful. Realize that all of the frantic activities that accompany the wedding day—the parties, celebrations, rehearsal, the ceremony itself—while being joyful events also take their toll of your emotional and nervous energy. The day is usually very crowded and you are bound to be quite tired as it closes. So don't try to cover a lot of miles before you come to the place where you will be spending the wedding night. You might even talk over whether that night is the best time for you to have your first experience of sexual relations. If you decide, as most couples will, that you want to make love on your wedding night, schedule plenty of time to relax and make sure there is no plane to catch early the next morning. The same relaxed pace should hold true for the rest of the honeymoon. Go somewhere that both of you will enjoy but make sure that you have plenty of time for each other.

FREQUENCY

Some couples ask about the proper frequency of marital relations and how long the acts involved should last. There is, of course, no general answer. Among happy, well-adjusted couples, frequency will vary according to mood, temperament, physical health, age, opportunity and many other factors. Some couples seem to have relations on a fairly regular, almost planned basis. With others, it is largely a matter of mood and impulse. As you learn to interpret each other's needs and desires, a mutually satisfactory pattern will emerge.

For some couples, intercourse almost daily in the early months of marriage is not unusual (although a little less often seems more typical). While relations almost three times a week after three or four years of marriage is an average that can be guessed at.

Again, the duration of sex relations is entirely a matter of a couple's mood and preference. Sometimes if both are in a special state of readiness, the whole process may not take more than ten or fifteen minutes. At other times, when the mood is slower, and more relaxed, an hour or more might not be too long.

AWKWARDNESS

Overcoming early awkwardness together and discovering how to please each other is an intimate, private joy that binds them more closely together. The first time your fiance kissed you was clumsy in comparison to the last, but there was something special about it that you remember tenderly. So it is with love-making in marriage.

Married couples can and should discuss physical love-making between themselves. It is good and proper for them to express their moods and feelings, thoughts and preferences. They learn to be frank and honest on a very intimate level and trust grows. If a temporary lack of response or an occasional desire to postpone intercourse should sometimes occur, they understand each other and do not misinterpret such occasions as rejection or decrease of love. Sexual love-making will be a deeply satisfying dimension of most marriages provided the partners do not demand too much too soon, of themselves, of each other, or of sexuality.

PREGNANCY

Some advise newly married couples to postpone first pregnancy until they are "fully adjusted." There is a danger in this suggestion because full adjustment like "total maturity" never happens. If a couple takes time to think about it and then mutually agrees to delay pregnancy for sound reasons, well and good. But be careful of the financial security trap which says, "We have to have this much space and that amount of money in the bank and then we will be secure and ready for a child." As material goods accumulate, yesterday's luxuries become today's necessities and the package of things "we absolutely need" get bigger and bigger.

Marital life is meant to be fruitful. Moving into parenthood continues the normal growth and development of husband and wife as persons and as lovers. Be careful of buying all the propaganda of the new generation, for sometimes it feeds an immature desire to prolong "early romance," and to play at marriage without confronting the reality that sex involves children and a deeper level of commitment to each other and to new life.

If the wife is in good health, there is no reason why marital relations should not be enjoyed in pregnancy up to a few weeks before delivery. By this time she will probably be consulting her doctor for checkups and his advice should be followed. After delivery a rest period of four to six weeks is usual before marital relations are resumed. Some length of time like this is required before the wife's reproductive organs resume their normal shape, tone and vitality.

During the time before and after birth, as well as any other periods when temporary abstinence from sexual relations is necessary or desirable, couples should exercise especially great consideration one for the other. For some, recalling insights gained from past experience, it might be wise to avoid those actions and situations which they know will produce intense stimulation and arousal, which could lead to discord and frustration.

Another question that might be added here is the advisability of intercourse during the menstrual period. There is really no medical or moral question involved. The sensibilities of the partners are the only consideration. In some instances, one or both partners may prefer, for esthetic reasons, not to have intercourse under these circumstances.

Remember, you and your partner are unique. There will never be another couple like you. Your sexual life is unique to your relationship. If it brings you satisfaction and enables you to express and receive love, it is alive and well and no cause for concern.

"Those who have money have trouble about it;

those who have not have trouble without it."

The pragmatic American says, "Time is money;" the wiser Latin says, "Money is only money, time is life itself." During your married life together it is entirely likely that you will acquire and dispose of over a third of a million dollars.

Money and Marriage

Money is an important factor in our lives that enters into most of our plans, dreams and calculations. It can be one of the most treacherous areas for adjustment even in the most loving marriages.

MONEY MEANS

The most important thing about money is the meaning it carries for you. Shortly after men stopped bartering furs for spears, they invented money as a convenient, symbolic means of exchange. Like all powerful symbols—the flag, a kiss, long hair, four-letter-words—money excites various strong emotions in each of us. For some people money can mean power, security, control, status, acceptance . . . the lack of money can mean inferiority, guilt, depression, anxiety. Because it encompasses so many possibilities for good and evil in our lives, money is one of the most basic of human motivations. Some people covet it. Others disdain it. Some worry about it constantly. Some still think it grows on trees.

How you feel about money, the meanings it carries for you and your partner will determine the levels of agreement you reach about how to use it. Each of you may have developed quite different attitudes conditioned by your earlier life experiences. Right now or very early in your marriage, these personal attitudes ought to be honestly explored and shared.

PAST INFLUENCES

Anyone who grew up in poverty where money for even basic essentials was not always available could easily develop great insecurities concerning it. Such a person might need to have "money in the bank," and other obvious signs of security . . . a home of his own and solid pieces of furniture. To him even minor expenditures on entertainment or frivolities could be very threatening. On the other hand, the person who comes from a fairly affluent home, who got everything he wanted most of the time, may take money for granted. He can't really worry about it too much and may even waste it foolishly.

Most of you will fall between these extremes, but you almost certainly have picked up some definite if more subtle attitudes about money. Here are some possibilities. Some of you had parents who carried thrift to extremes, who almost worshipped money as an end in itself and enjoyed nothing more than to see it pile up in the building and loan passbook. Perhaps in your home one parent held the privilege of controlling and dispensing all of the family resources and wielded this position like a club destroying any sense of partnership and participation. If your spouse should try something similar, you might be very resentful without ever knowing why.

Some of you might still be carrying echoes from a childhood when the deprivation of money meant punishment; or receiving money from parents was conditional upon conforming to ideas and behavior patterns you simply didn't agree with. Sometimes, not rarely, you find a husband who refuses to tell his wife how much he earns. His reasons can be various. Maybe he feels it helps keep her dependent. Possibly he is ashamed he does not earn more. Perhaps keeping her in the dark will allow him to spend more on things "every man has a right to."

BUY NOW

Our society is geared to make conspicuous consumers of us all. There are constant commercials beamed at your brain with their powerful, insistent message: Buy! Buy! Buy! "This cosmetic will make you beautiful. That deodorant will bring friends and acceptance. You deserve this hi-fi, boat, or snowmobile. You are shrewd if you buy this, upwardly mobile and with it if you buy that. You are a loser if you don't own a few of these." It is a rare person who isn't influenced by this incessant bombardment. The number of young couples who dig themselves into an economic hole through being unable to wait to purchase anything, is really very large.

REFLECTION

Take three minutes right now, maybe with a piece of paper and a pencil, and reflect on your background and attitudes concerning money. Try these questions: What does money mean to me? How do I feel about money? Why do I feel the way I do? A little contemplation of this kind can turn up some very interesting insights.

You might follow this with another three minute exercise during which you ask yourself: What does money mean to my partner? Try to make an educated guess about *his* or *her* thoughts, background and attitudes. These brief exercises can make you more sensitive to the whole area of finances.

HE LIKES, SHE LIKES, WE LIKE

In addition to individual differences there might well be masculine and feminine differences as to what each of you value. Try this. Dream for a moment about the things you hope to be able to save for in the next five years. Maybe each of you could make a list. Try to be honest and don't put down items just to please your partner.

George's list might include a car, (or better car), ski, bowling or fishing equipment, a power lawn mower, tools or even a workshop, a good steak at least once a week, tickets to sporting events, a fat savings account so "we won't be caught short," a home we own ourselves, a well stocked bar.

Susan's list might reflect feminine dreams. It could include drapery prints, attractive furniture, an adequate wardrobe, (with good suits and jewelry because "in the long run they are the better buys") a home or apartment that has some beauty in it, travel, rooms for children, a dishwasher, and enough put aside for regular visits to the beauty parlor.

These two divergent dreams are dependent on the same basic family income. How do you blend the dreams together? How do you think about income, expense and the future in order that dreams may become reality?

First of all talk long and honestly about your preferences, expectancies and priorities. See where they fit together, where compromises may have to be effected and where allowances may have to be made for something the other partner wants that you are not really interested in at all.

A PROCESS

Set up a process for dealing with money matters. Who is going to handle the money? Will one of you be chiefly responsible or will it be a strictly fifty-fifty approach? Will each of you have some amount you can dispose of independently? When will you talk about money? "Incessantly." "Every four years, whether we need to or not." "Only when we run short." "The first of every month, at 7:31 p.m." "Oh, we'll get around to it sometime."

Get some of the pamphlets or booklets which banks, savings and loans and insurance companies distribute, or buy a budget book. These items can stimulate thinking and help you to devise a money plan. But remember, nobody has the precise plan that fits your dreams, hopes and temperaments. You are going to have to shape your own over a period of time.

Consider the time factor. Your earning capacities will probably increase but so will your expenditures. The value of the dollar will probably go down. Savings put aside on a regular and disciplined basis can be very valuable. As time passes, the things you think important will change, so build in flexibility. There are certain to be emergencies. Allow for them, but don't live in fear of them. Where do you fit between these two views of tomorrow: "Spend now and let tomorrow take care of itself," or "Scrimp and save. We will begin to live at the age of forty-seven."

As you work out a plan, be sure it is mutually agreed upon and realistic. If it isn't realistic you won't have the discipline to carry it out. If it isn't mutually agreed on, one party or the other will soon drift away from it. Some money experts say that keeping careful track of all income and expenditures for the first three to six months of a marriage is most important in providing a realistic basis for future planning. But don't fall into the *accounting trap.* The fact that you can account for every penny after it has been spent does not make you a good money-manager.

TAKE INVENTORY

Now, before marriage, sum up your present financial situation. Try to be as candid as you can with yourself and each other. Include the eighty dollars you may still owe on last year's vacation or sports jacket. You may be tempted to say, "Oh, I won't mention that. I'll take care of it myself." But be careful. Little traps like this may come back to haunt you.

Put down your assets: Cash on hand, savings, securities, clothing which is still serviceable, jewelry, sports equipment, household equipment, car, furnishings, furniture, insurance, any guaranteed increase in income, etc. etc. List your liabilities, too, including bills owed, installment payments, outstanding loans, medical bills, any immediate obligations to parents, the costs of the wedding and the honeymoon. Do your very best to clean up all your debts before marriage. Couples who marry in the shadow of substantial debt need an exceptional spirit of sacrifice and discipline.

CREDIT?

Be wary of credit cards and credit buying. Buying on credit can be a great boon. It is often a major disaster. Use it carefully and wisely. Study the alternatives. Know what it costs you to buy on credit. Be sure you know what you are doing and that you really want and can use the item before undertaking credit obligations. Remember credit cards are a wonderful convenience, but for some people they take on a quality of unreality, like play money, and make spending very, very easy.

THE WORKING WIFE

Before World War II, very few women worked outside the home. Now the vast majority of young brides plan to work for some time after the wedding. This is quite understandable because the extra income is most useful. It may even be a temporary necessity if the husband is in service or completing his education. For some young women actively involved in a satisfying job or a profession, the stimulus of having something to do and the continued contact with friends and co-workers is prized for it prevents the sense of isolation and lack of purpose which some might experience sitting around a small apartment most of the day. Yet the argument for working wives is not all one-sided. Each couple ought to think about and discuss its implications for their marriage.

Some considerations: Does she really want to work? Many girls do. Some few just say they do because they presume their husbands expect it of them. Others might decide working is a good idea because they simply have no conception of what they would do if they did not keep a job. Sewing, cooking, shopping, decorating, reading, studying, involving themselves in projects and the community around them might seem appealing to some and appalling to others. Perhaps part-time work or volunteer work might be the better answer for some.

Have you ever reflected that if both husband and wife are working full-time jobs—forty, forty-five hours a week—courtesy, concern and simple justice say that the man should make a significant contribution to doing the household chores: (all of them?) dishwashing, laundry, vacuuming, cooking, grocery shopping, whatever.

Another thought: to what extent does the second salary create an artificial standard of living? Many couples start out by saying, "Well, she'll work 'x' number of months and then quit a few weeks before the baby is born. "Some get very used to that second salary and begin to postpone pregnancy for such a length of time that their values can get pretty distorted. Then, if the young wife does get pregnant earlier than planned, the fact of giving up income may lead both to regard approaching parenthood as a burden rather than a joy. One very important suggestion: if the wife does work, very little (or better, none) of her salary should be used to meet the daily expenses.

The wife's income is not all profit. Consider: her income tax; her loss as a dependent deduction on her husband's income tax; the cost of the special wardrobe she needs for work; transportation, lunches, various dues, fees and pools; the services that may have to be purchased, cleaning, mending, washing, prepared foods, because the wife has less time to devote to these tasks.

Most significant of all for some couples is the physical and emotional drain of eight-hour work days which might send home two tired and edgy people to work on the relationship of marriage. The working wife is part of the American scene but this does not make it an unmixed blessing.

GENEROSITY

Having laid out some thoughts on sound family economics, there is a kind of creeping feeling of uneasiness. Too many individuals and couples could use the foregoing as a blueprint for self-centeredness.

Remember the old adage: "Whatever you own, owns you; the more you possess, the more you are possessed." The things you own and care about demand time, attention, worry, anxiety, care and upkeep. Be wary lest you become slaves to a house, a lawn, a savings account.

As life is only fully possessed when it is shared, so too, goods, the things we have, the blessings given us must also be shared. There are many people in far greater need than you, likely not very far from you. From the first day of marriage, think about which of all the worthy causes—community, international, medical, church support, missions, youth, children—have some appeal for you and help them. You might go beyond this if you will to "unworthy causes." One of the very basic differences between Christ's teaching on loving and helping others and some of the distortions that have crept into Christianity is simply that the Christian tries to help those that are in need, not because they pledge to clean up, shape up, become productive, vote right or anything else, but simply because they are human beings in need.

Maybe your sense of generosity and sharing will take the form of money donations to causes, maybe it will become far more personal and seek out individual people you can help. Or maybe still, you will spend some of your substance in babysitters, travel, equipment so that you as a couple work at some service projects. This might be the best sharing of all.

START TALKING NOW

Work through the lists and questions on the next two pages and discuss how they might apply to the first year of your marriage.

DISCUSSION STARTERS

Housing

What kind? Where? Near what? Near whom? Too near whom? Short-term or long-term? Own or rent? What's included in the rental package—heating, utilities, phone, electricity, water? What about decorating, maintenance, insurance, even things like garbage pickup and snow removal?

Furnishings

How do you feel about your home? What do you (both) want it to be: a castle? a showcase? a retreat? a funhouse?—warm and cozy or modern and functional? a combination? or just an address? Your home should reflect both of your tastes, personalities and life styles. It should live and grow with you so you don't have to make all decisions now. Your home is dreams and shared experiences. But it is also planning, hard comparison shopping and such dull things as checking warranties, interest on loans and credit ratings.

Furnishings can include anything from major equipment such as stoves, washers, and such like right down to the furniture for each room including hassocks and bookcases.

Appliances

Sewing machines, hairdryer, television, clock, clock-radio, vacuum cleaner, osterizer. Some questions: What will you bring from the family attic or from your own previous apartments? Which items do you need first? Which can you do without entirely?

Software

Towels, sheets, shower curtains, slip covers, bedspreads, etc. etc.

Decorative Items

Rugs, lamps, pictures, ashtrays, everything from psychedelic posters to bowling trophies. Question: Do you want to bring many of these things with you? Would this perhaps be a good time to throw a lot of things away?

Household Supplies

Mops, pails, tools, brooms, dishcloths, ladders, cleaning supplies, dishes, pots and pans, knives and forks, paper items—everything from plates to shelf covering.

Menu planning. That's one thousand-ninety-times-a-year excluding snacks. It's not just having him over a couple of times as before marriage, and blowing half the budget on a sirloin just to impress him. What about variety, preferences, new dishes, left-overs and preparation time if you are both working.

Consider things like shopping expertise. Where you buy, the brands, and sizes! What about weekly specials? Budget stretchers? Delivery charges? Can you make a list and stick to it? Then there is the entertaining of friends and relatives, parties, liquor, dining out, special lunches.

Clothing

What's on hand? How long will it last? What clothing will you need to buy in the next year? What about the never-ending cleaning, laundry and repair bills? How do you stay in style and still not end up with too many Nehru jackets?

Personal Supplies

Everything from, cosmetics to toothpaste to cigarettes to lifesavers.

Transportation

What will bus and train fares amount to? How long will the present car last? What kind of car do you need? How big? How small? New? Used? What about payments, license, depreciation, trade-in value, repairs, fuel, insurance, parking availability, parking cost?

Job Expenses

Union dues, collections, special equipment, special clothing, uniforms, travel, etc., etc.

Insurance

Life, property, liability, health, term, major medical, accident, Blue Cross. This topic is a maze. Shop around, compare, get advice you can trust.

Health

Doctors, dentists, therapists, medicines, hospitalization.

Education

The husband's, the wife's, the couple's, the children's. Books, school fees, tuition, lectures, subscriptions, etc.

Recreation

Clubs, movies, dinner, entertaining, theater, parking, baby-sitters, newspapers, magazines, hi-fi, books, vacations, special clothes, home entertainment—how often, with whom? Sports equipment, tickets, fees, travel.

Miscellaneous

This category could go on forever. Gifts, Christmas cards, community projects, memberships, etc., etc., etc.

And after everything else come taxes, taxes, taxes!!!

"Two people in love set requirements for each other, demands on each other so remarkable, that no law-giver on earth would dare inflict them on his fellows."

A Note on Law and Marriage

Your marriage is the most *intimate* of relationships, your future family will be the most personal of love communities. Yet, neither marriage nor family are merely private affairs. They are also public institutions.

The fact that you are married and the kind of marriage you build both have consequences for society. The well-being of your marriage and family require support from society. They require the services of governmental, civil and social agencies from schools and police forces to health departments and dog catchers. The family needs society; on the other hand, society needs good families for the ordering of human relations and the nurturing and rearing of children who will become citizens. Thus, for its own good and the good of its members, the state establishes laws regulating and supporting marriage and family life.

You are also a member of the church, which is not only the People of God infused with the Holy Spirit but also a visible society which needs to identify its members in order to preach the Gospel to them and to involve them in its liturgical and sacramental life. To make certain its members are ready to understand and participate in the Christian dimensions of marriage, as relationship, as new status and office in the church, as re-presentation of the mystery of Christ's love, the church, too, establishes regulations concerning marriage.

Please don't become impatient with the paperwork required. Laws are a good idea. If all men were responsible, wise, noble and completely unselfish, there would be no need for law. But because we are sometimes uninformed, irresponsible and selfish, laws are established by the long experience of mankind to tell us clearly the limits beyond which we cannot go without hurting ourselves, another person or society.

AGE

Church law stipulates that a young man may not enter a true marriage before his sixteenth birthday, or a young lady before her fourteenth birthday. These ages seem far too young to us and indeed in our complex society they are. They were far more suitable for Romeo and Juliet and their friends in the Middle Ages, because life was so much simpler. Most people began their families much earlier and died before the age of 40.

Today the church abides by the minimal age laws of the various states, usually 18 for the boy and 16 for the girl, and will not sanction the marriages of younger people.

PREVIOUS MARRIAGE

According to church law, a person who has been involved in a prior, valid marriage is incapable of contracting another true and valid marriage while the first partner is alive, if no annulment of the first marriage has been granted. If either you or your fiance have ever been involved in a previous marriage of any type, the parish priest who is working with you should be consulted immediately so that the party's freedom to marry may be checked out.

IMPOTENCE

One of the essential requirements of marriage is the ability to perform the act of sexual intercourse. Any person who for psychological or physical reasons is incapable of doing so is called impotent and not able to enter a valid marriage. Notice, sterility and impotence are not the same problem. There are many couples, who while able to have sexual relations cannot conceive children for a variety of medical reasons. These couples, called sterile, are permitted to marry.

MARRIAGE BETWEEN RELATIVES

There are church laws about marriages between relatives. People may be related either by "blood" or by marriage. Blood relatives are forbidden to marry anyone up to the third degree of descent from a common ancestor, that is, up to and inclusive of second cousins.

Relatives by marriage cannot marry anyone in the direct line of descent. The appropriate authority may grant a dispensation from these prohibitions for certain degrees of relationship.

CONSENT

In order to enter a true marriage, a person must understand and freely consent to the terms of the marriage contract. The church is very concerned lest anyone enter marriage against his will. Some of the factors it lists that prevent true consent are as follows:

1. Lack of the use of reason, as when a person is much too young, intoxicated or drugged, or suffering from mental illness.

2. Ignorance of what marriage normally entails also impairs consent, e.g., the exchange or rights to sexual intercourse, a common life, mutual support, etc.

3. Duress and fear. A person who is forced to marry another under threat of injury or death is, of course, not consenting freely.

4. Pretense, fictitious consent, or mistaken identity.

THE CEREMONY

The church also sets up certain conditions for the ceremony, the celebration of marriage. For Catholics, "Only those marriages are valid which are contracted by the pastor, the bishop of the diocese or a priest or deacon delegated by either of these, and at least two witnesses."

The priest who officiates at your wedding does not administer the sacrament of matrimony. He is there as the official witness representing the church community. The bride and groom confer the sacrament upon each other in the exchange of their conjugal promises. In this official, public, religious act, you are the ministers of grace, one to another.

THE PAPERWORK

You will normally be required to secure baptismal and confirmation certificates and to fill out questionnaires concerning: your freedom to marry, your consent, your understanding of the meaning of marriage, the responsibilities of husband and wife, and the duties of parents to children. The priest provides these questionnaires and helps you fill them out.

Sometimes there are affidavits required if one or both parties are unknown to the priest. Here friends or relatives of the bride or groom will be requested to testify as to their freedom and ability to marry. Again, these forms are available at the rectory and the priest who has been through this procedure numerous times will suggest how the whole thing can be taken care of most easily.

THE BANNS

Normally on three successive Sundays or feast days, your intention to marry will be announced at Mass, usually at the church of the bride and the church of the groom.

STATE LAWS ON MARRIAGE

THE MARRIAGE LICENSE: All states require that persons wishing to marry obtain legal permission to do so and that the fact of the marriage be recorded. This is the purpose of the marriage license. In most states it is issued by the county recorder or some other county officer. Most states require a short waiting period between the time you obtain a license and the marriage itself.

PHYSICAL EXAMINATION: Many states have laws forbidding marriage of those suffering from venereal disease. These states often require a blood test of the partners shortly before the issuing of the license. This can almost certainly be done by the family physician who is quite familiar with the procedures.

SOCIAL CUSTOMS

From the caveman who probably developed a special grip to drag his bride by the hair to her new home to the horn-tooting crepe-paper decorated cars you can see on the streets of any city on a Saturday afternoon, marriage and the events that preceded it have always been surrounded by a variety of customs. These have invariably involved the friends and the families of the engaged couples. Beyond that they vary considerably from rural area to big city, from very traditional to far out, from quite simple to remarkably elaborate. Some weddings have rich, ethnic overtones and everybody instinctively knows his role. Some are given over to wedding directors who shape up the whole situation. There are numerous booklets that cover all these matters if you are in the mood to consult them.

Here let's just make several simple points:

1) Your wedding is not just a private affair. It is a time of fulfillment, rejoicing, celebration for families and friends, too. (If you are a girl, about three hours after your birth your mother was likely phantasizing what your wedding would be like.) So some discussion and consideration of their feelings and preferences is in order.

2) Help each other with the planning. If you're a man, don't leave it all to the bride-to-be. She needs your support.

3) Use common sense about the amount of money—yours and other people's—you intend to spend. Be especially careful of the bridesmaids and their budgets. Make it a good party, but you really don't need an extravaganza.

To celebrate is to demonstrate the meaning of some joyful event—by dramatizing it with actions, words, rituals and music that underline and heighten its importance.

Your wedding day is a significant, joyous event for you, your families and the Christian community. It is the beginning of the long adventure of Christian marriage and merits great celebration.

Celebrate Your Wedding Day

Contemporary liturgical forms for the marriage rite are quite flexible. You have many options as to the readings, prayers and actions you might like to use. May we encourage you to study the choices, talk them over with the parish priest and fashion a set of ceremonies that will make your wedding day a memorable expression of your unique love for each other.

Notice . . . because of local customs and circumstances, individual parishes may differ concerning the days or times of marriage, the musical, floral and photographic arrangements and other matters. The parish priest will explain the local situations to you and apprise you of any special resources that may be available to assist you.

YOUR WEDDING MASS

The ideal setting for the sacrament of matrimony is as an integral part of the Mass, the Eucharistic celebration. It is strongly recommended that inter-faith marriages, too, take place at Mass.

What follows is an outline of the wedding ceremony and a listing of the options available to you.

Procession

The ceremony begins with the entrance procession. The priest, attendants, witnesses, parents of the bride, parents of the groom and others may take part in the procession. Consider the arrangement you prefer and work out a chart for the wedding march. An entrance song is to be sung at this time; however, it may be replaced by some other suitable piece of music.

The bride, groom and attendants go to their assigned places either within the sanctuary (altar area) or just in front of it, depending on the design of the church and local custom.

THE LITURGY OF THE WORD

The Mass begins as usual except that there are four different versions of the opening prayer—each mentioning the bride and groom by name and asking God's blessing on their love.

OPENING PRAYER

A

Father, You have made the bond of marriage a holy mystery, a symbol of Christ's love for His Church. Hear our prayers for N. and N. With faith in You and in each other they pledge their love today. May their lives always bear witness to the reality of that love.

B

Father, hear our prayers for N. and N. who today are united in marriage before Your altar.

Give them Your blessing, and strengthen their love for each other.

C

Father, when You created mankind You willed that man and wife should be one.

Bind N. and N. in the loving union of marriage; and make their love fruitful so that they may be living witnesses to Your divine love in the world.

D

Almighty God, hear our prayers for N. and N. who have come here today to be united in the sacrament of marriage.

Increase their faith in You and in each other, and through them bless Your Church (with Christian children).

The Scripture Readings

There are three scripture readings. The first from the Old Testament, the second from the Epistles, the third from the Gospels. What follows is a list of references to the various permitted readings. You can, of course, find them in any Bible. Look them up, read them over and choose the one reading in each group that is most meaningful to you.

There are also a variety of very brief responsory prayers and Alleluia verses that come between the Epistle and Gospel.

OLD TESTAMENT READINGS

Genesis 1:26-28,31a	Male and female He created.
Genesis 2:18-24	Two in one flesh.
Genesis 24:48-51,58-67	Isaac loved Rebecca.
Tobit 7:9c-10,11c-17	May God join you together.
Tobit 8:5-10	May God bring us to old age.
Song of Songs 2:8-10,14,16a	Love is strong as death.
Ecclesiasticus 26:1-4,16-21	The good wife.
Jeremiah 31:31-32a,33-34a	I will make a new covenant.

EPISTLES

Romans 8:31b-35,37-39	The love of Christ.
Romans 12:1-2,9,18	Your new mind in Christ.
I Corinthians 6-13c,15a,17-20	Your body is a temple.
I Corinthians 12:31,13:8a	Nothing profits without love.
Ephesians 5:2a,21-33	As with Christ and His Church.
Colossians 3:12-17	Love, the bond of perfection.
1 Peter 3:1-9	Love the brethren.
1 John 3:18-24	Love is to be real and active.
1 John 4:7-12	God is love.
Revelation 19:1,5-9a	The bride of the lamb.

GOSPELS

Matthew 5:1-12	Rejoice, your reward is great.
Matthew 5:13-16	The light of the world.
Matthew 7:21,24-29	The house built on rock.
Matthew 19:3-6	What God has joined together.
Matthew 22:35-40	The greatest commandment.
Mark 10:6-9	No longer two but one body.
John 2:1-11	The wedding feast at Cana.
John 15:9-12	Remain in my love.
John 15:12-16	Love one another.
John 17:20-26	May they be completely one.

Notice, the first two readings need not be done by a priest. Perhaps the fathers of the bride and groom could each read one, or some members of the wedding party or other close friends could be invited to participate in this manner.

After the Gospel the priest will deliver an appropriate homily.

THE EXCHANGE OF VOWS

As you know, the priest does not administer the Sacrament of Matrimony. He is simply official witness for the Church. By the solemn exchange of vows the bride and groom bestow the sacrament, one upon the other.

The priest introduces this phase of the ceremony with a short statement on the purpose of marriage. Then bride and groom are questioned about their freedom of choice, fidelity to each other and their acceptance of children. Each is called upon to answer the questions separately.

Following this the bride and groom each publicly pronounce their vows and declare and affirm their intention to take each other in marriage:

"I, John, take you, Mary, to be my wife. I promise to be true to you in good times and in bad, in sickness and in health, I will love you and honor you all the days of my life."

Finally, after witnessing their consent, the priest blesses the solemn covenant in the name of the people of God.

So long as the key elements outlined here are clearly present, the couple may modify the language of the vows or add appropriate elements that have special meaning for them.

Blessing of Rings

The vows may be exchanged with the couple facing the priest, facing each other or facing the community. As an enduring symbol of their marriage the wedding rings are blessed by the priest and then exchanged by the bride and the groom while reciting a further declaration of love and fidelity. There are three prayers to choose from.

BLESSING OF RINGS

A

Lord, bless + and consecrate N.
and N. in their love for each other.
May these rings be a symbol of true
faith in each other, and always re-
mind them of their love.

B

May the Lord bless + these rings
which you give to each other as the
sign of your love and fidelity.

C

Lord, bless these rings which we
bless + in Your name. Grant that
those who wear them may always
have a deep faith in each other.
May they do Your will and always
live together in peace, good will,
and love.

Prayer of the Faithful

Immediately following the ceremony, the entire congregation
joins in the prayer of the faithful addressing petitions to God
on behalf of the newly married couple. There are several
forms for this prayer available; or it may be done
spontaneously with members of the congregation expressing
their personal sentiments. If you wish, special petitions may
be composed for the occasion.

LITURGY OF THE EUCHARIST

The new Mass rite suggests an offertory procession in which
the bread and wine are brought to the altar. This could be
done by the bride and groom themselves, by parents,
members of the wedding or other pre-determined members
of the congregation. There are three different versions of the
prayer over the gifts.

PRAYER OVER THE GIFTS

A

Lord, accept our offering for this
newly-married couple, N. and N.
By Your love and providence You
have brought them together; now
bless them all the days of their
married life.

B

Lord, accept the gifts we offer You
on this happy day.

In Your Fatherly love watch over
and protect N. and N. whom You
have united in marriage.

C

Lord, hear our prayers and accept
the gifts we offer for N. and N.
Today You have made them one in
the sacrament of marriage. May
the mystery of Christ's unselfish
love, which we celebrate in this
eucharist, increase their love for
You and for each other.

Next comes the preface. Three variant forms.

PREFACE

A

Father, all-powerful and ever-living God, we do well always and everywhere to give You thanks. By this sacrament Your grace unites man and woman in an unbreakable bond of love and peace.

You have designed the chaste love of husband and wife for the increase of the human family and of Your own family born in baptism.

You are the loving Father of the world of nature; You are the loving Father of the new creation of grace. In Christian marriage You bring together the two orders of creation: Nature's gift of children enriches the world, Your grace enriches Your Church.

Through Christ the choirs of angels and all the saints praise and worship Your glory. May our voices blend with theirs as we join in their unending hymn:

B

Father, all-powerful, and everliving God, we do well always and everywhere to give You thanks.

You created man in love to share Your divine life. We see his high destiny in the love of husband and wife, which bears the imprint of Your own divine love.

Love is man's origin, love is his constant calling, love is his fulfillment in heaven.

The love of man and woman is made holy in the sacrament of marriage, and becomes the mirror of Your everlasting love.

Through Christ the choirs of angels and all the saints praise and worship Your glory. May our voices blend with theirs as we join in their unending hymn:

C

Father, all-powerful and everliving God, we do well always and everywhere to give You thanks through Jesus Christ our Lord.

Through Him You entered into a new covenant with Your people. You restored man to grace in the saving mystery of redemption. You gave him a share in divine life through his union with Christ. You made him an heir of Christ's eternal glory.

This outpouring of love in the new covenant of grace is symbolized in the marriage covenant that seals the love of husband and wife and reflects Your divine plan of love.

And so, with the angels and all the saints in heaven we proclaim Your glory and join in their unending hymn of praise:

The mass proceeds as usual until after the congregational recitation of the Our Father. At this point the solemn nuptial blessing is bestowed by the priest on the newly married couple. Again, three texts are available, choose the one you like.

NUPTIAL BLESSING

A

My dear friends, let us ask God for His continued blessings upon this bridegroom and his bride (or N. and N.).

Holy Father, creator of the universe, maker of man and woman in Your own likeness, source of blessing for married life, we humbly pray to You for this woman who today is united with her husband in this sacrament of marriage.

May Your fullest blessing come upon her and her husband so that together they may rejoice in Your gift of married love (and enrich Your Church with their children).

Lord, may they both praise You when they are happy and turn to You in their sorrows. May they be glad that You help them in their need.

May they pray to You in the community of the Church, and be Your witnesses in the world. May they reach old age in the company of their friends, and come at last to the kingdom of heaven.

B

My dear friends, let us turn to the Lord and pray that He Will bless with His grace this woman (or N.) now married in Christ to this man (or N.) and that (through the sacrament of the body and blood of Christ) He will unite in love the couple He has joined in this holy bond.

Father, by Your power You have made everything out of nothing. In the beginning You created the universe and made mankind in Your own likeness. You gave man the constant help of woman so that man and woman should no longer be two, but one flesh, and You teach us that what You have united may never be divided.

Father, You have made the union of man and wife so holy a mystery that it symbolizes the marriage of Christ and His Church.

Father, by Your plan man and woman are united, and married life has been established as the one blessing that was not forfeited by original sin or washed away in the flood.

Look with love upon this woman, Your daughter, now joined to her husband in marriage. She asks Your blessing. Give her the grace of love and peace. May she always follow the example of the holy women whose praises are sung in the scriptures.

May her husband put his trust in her and recognize that she is his equal and heir with him to the life of grace. May he always honor her and love her as Christ loves His bride, the Church.

Father, keep them always true to Your commandments. Keep them faithful in marriage and let them be living examples of Christian life.

Give them the strength which comes from the gospel so that they may be witnesses of Christ to others. (Bless them with children and help them to be good parents.

May they live to see their children's children.) And, after a happy old age, grant them fullness of life with the saints in the kingdom of heaven.

C

Let us pray to the Lord for N. and N. who come to God's altar at the beginning of their married life so that they may always be united in love for each other (as they now share in the body and blood of Christ).

Holy Father, You created mankind in Your own image and made man and woman to be joined as husband and wife in union of body and heart and so fulfill their mission in this world.

Father, to reveal the plan of Your love, You made the union of husband and wife an image of the covenant between You and Your people. In the fulfillment of this sacrament, the marriage of Christian man and woman is a sign of the marriage between Christ and Church. Father, stretch out Your hand, and bless N. and N.

Lord, grant that as they begin to live this sacrament they may share with each other the gifts of Your love, and become one in heart and mind, as witnesses to Your presence in their marriage. Help them to create a home together (and give them children to be formed by the gospel who will have a place in Your family).

Give Your blessings to (N.) Your daughter, may she be a good wife and mother, caring for the home, faithful in love for her husband, generous and kind. Give Your blessings to (N.) Your son, so that he may be a faithful husband and a good father.

Father, grant that as they come together to Your table on earth, so they may one day have the joy of sharing Your feast in heaven.

Peace Greeting

Immediately after the blessing comes the greeting of peace. With some appropriate gesture such as a hand shake, the priest bestows a sign of love and peace upon the bride and groom. At this time they are invited to exchange a sign with each other . . . perhaps an embrace or formal kiss and then to extend this "peace greeting" to the other members of the wedding and to the congregation, again with whatever sign they deem appropriate.

Communion

The newly married couple has the option of receiving Holy Communion under both species—the consecrated bread and wine from the chalice. They receive immediately after the priest. There are three optional forms of the prayers after communion.

PRAYER AFTER COMMUNION

A

Lord, in Your love You have given us this eucharist to unite us with one another and with You. As You have made N. and N. one in this sacrament of marriage (and in the sharing of the one bread and the one cup), so now make them one in love for each other.

B

Lord, we who have shared the food of Your table pray for our friends N. and N. whom You have joined together in marriage. Keep them close always. May their love for each other proclaim to all the world their faith in You.

C

Almighty God, may the sacrifice we have offered and the eucharist we have shared strengthen the love of N. and N., and give us all Your Fatherly aid.

At the end of Mass the priest pronounces a final blessing over the couple about to go forth into the years of their life together. There are three optional texts.

FINAL BLESSING

A

May the Lord Jesus, Who was guest at the wedding in Cana, bless you in your families and your friends. Amen.

May Jesus, Who loved His Church to the very end fill your hearts with His love always. Amen.

May He grant that, as you believe in His resurrection, so you may await Him in joy and hope. Amen.
May almighty God bless you all, the Father, and the Son, + and the Holy Spirit. Amen.

B

God the eternal Father keep you in love with each other, so that the peace of Christ may stay with you and be always in your home. Amen.
May (your children bless you) your friends console you and all men live in peace with you. Amen.

May you always bear witness to the love of God in this world so that the afflicted and the needy will find you generous friends, and welcome you into the joys of heaven. Amen.

May almighty God bless you all, the Father, and the Son, + and the Holy Spirit. Amen.

C

May God, the almighty Father, give you His joy and bless you (in your children). Amen.

May the only Son of God have mercy on you and help you both in good times and in bad. Amen.
May the Holy Spirit of God fill your hearts with His love always. Amen.

May almighty God bless you all, the Father, and the Son, + and the Holy Spirit. Amen.

The ceremony concludes with the recessional.